The Entrepreneurial Toolkit

How to hyper-grow your business + get stuff done quickly, cheaply

and ultra-efficiently.

by Tim Levy

July 2013

Title: *The Entrepreneurial Handbook*

Subtitle: *How to hyper-grow your business + get stuff done quickly, cheaply and ultra-efficiently.*

Author: *Tim Levy*

Published by: *Tim Levy and Associates LLC*

First Edition, 2013.

Published in the United States of America

Dedication

This book is dedicated to my amazing and lovely family. My life would be incomplete without my Bella, Finn, Zak and Angela. Love you guys!

Contents

Introduction

My Story

I didn't know how lucky I was until many years later. As a young boy my father invited all these CEOs of multi-million dollar companies to my kitchen table!

They would talk about entrepreneurial ideas, what to delegate and what not to, strategies to get more out of their employees, how to bring their valuable products and services to people in their market, and how to be good stewards of those profits. I thought everybody grew up this way…with this "mindset of the wealthy".

I didn't realize most people grow up without the benefit of this "masterminding with captains of industry". They have one or two parents around and usually there's little talk of profits and business growth. It's more "how to pay the bills" and "get an education and a good job" type talk. This philosophy makes many people comfortable later in life. But many also yearn to do and be something more. These people want to be remembered for the improvement they made in the lives of others.

Being around these CEOs, guys running businesses turning over say $20 to $50 million a year, shaped who I am and how I think. I didn't even know my good fortune. I just figured I was growing up the way any other kid does. My father was extraordinary in this way. He's still my #1 mastermind buddy to this day. He's been extraordinary for all the CEOs and business thinking he brought into my world. He's one out of twenty-three people in the Australian FCA Franchising Hall of Fame. Franchising is another word for taking a specific business system (an exact system for doing business) packaging it, expanding it by selling specific territorial or other rights to individual operators. So my access to elite minds and influence shaped the success I've had to this point in my life.

This access gave me the confidence to be a very young CEO. My family members have been CEOs for a long time. My brother is in big business, and my father's been in big business. My father was the Australian CEO of a major multi-national company for 9 years. Then he ran the Australian arm of a global network of CEOs that was very active, so we had these business leaders and high-level thinkers in our lives from my earliest days. I was constantly surrounded by them. Now I coach CEOs to be entrepreneurial thinkers. I also coach some fantastic entrepreneurs, helping them create then mastermind their strategy, working with them on a daily basis.

My Career

My career is split in two parts. In the first part, I pursued a conservative path. I had a fulltime job at a bricks and mortar business. I had the desk and the computer inside the cubicle.

I always felt the best in the world was happening in Silicon Valley because my interests were technology, creativity, music videos, picture films and Pixar.

For example, I remember when I got hired by IBM to do a job for their company event. I had to do a video to get and hold the attention of a jaded IBM sales crew. Between me and my point man at IBM, we had to motivate them to go out, kick ass and take names for IBM that year.

We knew the importance and power of sound. Therefore, we used big banging drums in a specific beat and cadence to get the attendees' attention. We used those drums strategically throughout the presentation to regain attention and 'amp up' the audience's concentration.

The Biggest Takeaway from my Early Business Career

The biggest takeaway, however, was that I noticed the video IBM wanted from me was effectively *repurposing an American video*. I just took out the American accent, put in Australian accents, substituted a Sydney setting for the American San Francisco setting and IBM loved it. This experience taught me how powerful and profitable repurposing or improving on an existing idea can be. This work confirmed for me that big things were happening in Silicon Valley.

Soon after, I left Australia. It was 1994. I was twenty two, and found a thriving economy in Silicon Valley that was very entrepreneurial.

Specifically, what I loved about America was the difference in attitude toward new ideas and innovation. They would say "yes" before they said "no", if you had an idea. People would go, "Great! HOW are we going to do it?"

Back in Australia, the conservative mindset says, "Ahh, well that sounds nice but risky." Or, "I did something like that but it didn't work and have you thought of this?" Aussies would shoot down ideas before even giving them a proper test. I just wasn't how I was thinking.

In America I moved up quickly to become a very young executive. I moved up to art director, then to creative director. At this point I was working with mainly Fortune 500 clients. So, I was working for brands including IBM, Acer, 3Com, Hewlett Packard, Sony and more. These were heady days for a twenty-something out of Sydney's north shore!

I was constantly looking at and doing design work, communication work, websites, CDs, videos and often strategy for these new products. Who remembers the old model of an IPO in Silicon Valley? In it, you worked crazy hours for a year or two or three. You'd get the product into the market, see if it worked, launch the IPO on the stock market and see if you could get *times ten* your money back on that first day your company's stock trades. That was the plan, at least!

This was before the nasty 2001 NASDAQ stock market crash. This was a time when internet businesses were scorching hot. Venture capital companies were so excited about internet businesses that they'd throw millions at these companies with little, if any demonstrable profit!

How I Discovered this System...In the Trenches

These were formative years for me. I had the chance to try out my ideas, tools, processes and strategies with live clients. That's how I discovered the ideas I'm sharing with you in this book.

Each industry has its unique challenges. I've consulted CEOs of a wide variety of businesses from plastic injection molding to large format printing. I've consulted with companies focusing on everything from self-storage to children's books to ad agencies and law firms. The same principles are still engrained in their thinking and businesses processes... the old way.

My client coaching and consulting work keeps me on the cutting edge. This works is exciting and fulfilling because it allows me to constantly polish and update my tools, tactics and processes. I get to try them out in the real world, at scale, from the very first moment. This, in turn, allows me to bring these techniques to you.

And I don't just apply these techniques to my clients. I've applied this system to create my own projects in books, albums, DVDs, TV shows, and stage shows. I was bitten by the entertainment bug early on and it doesn't show any signs of stopping. I'm still active in television, radio and print.

But there's a big problem with most creative types and artists. When I say creative types, I'm talking about painters, musicians, writers, or anyone with an idea. They have strong *right-brain* skills so they spend years on their manuscripts because creation is their great strength and comfort zone.

Often, however, they have **zero** business structural skills. This means that while they might having amazing art or songs or books or business ideas, they've not great at bringing them to market. They're often close to flat broke also. Can you relate?

To make matters worse, these right brain creative can be perfectionists, too. They spend lots of time on their manuscripts or product development trying to get it *just so*. "It's not quite right" or "just a little bit more, then I'll start selling it" are things they often say. This leads to investing way too much of their time and money into ideas the market won't pay for (or won't pay enough for to make it worthwhile).

This system is about changing all that. It's about cutting short the cycle of perfectionism. It's about avoiding the horrible fate of investing too much time and money into an idea the market won't pay for. I know what I'm talking about here because I did it, too!

Now, however, a few decades down the road, I do it differently. I'd like this book to be your shortcut. I'm a creative who's developed business skills through lots of sweat. So please, take advantage of this knowledge and experience. Please, learn and use these tools so you don't have to go through what I went through.

Example / Publishing Industry Power Shifts to...

Let's use the publishing industry as an example. Big publishing houses bank on the fact that writers don't know how to do business for themselves. So traditionally, the publishing house owned:

- product development

- marketing

- distribution, and therefore

- most all the profits.

Look how that business has changed now that those means of distribution are in the hands of authors. The tools I'll demonstrate can be used by anybody with a little willingness to learn. If you can point and click in a browser and type (or pay someone to type as you dictate) you can use these tools.

Look also at how the music business has changed. I don't need a big production budget, and I don't need hundreds of thousands of dollars in studio time to record my first album any more. I can do it on my laptop.

By the way, I don't want to give you the impression that the book or music publishing industries are bad. They're actually full of awesome people trying to genuinely help struggling artists. It's just that the world has changed. This book is about leveraging those changes to your immediate advantage.

These types of bootstrapping tactics are what this "fast to market, low time and money invested" system is all about.

Why Failing Quickly is the Secret of the Wealthy

So why you should listen to me about taking your idea and making it a business reality, or junking it fast because the market doesn't want it?

You should pay attention because *time is the only truly scarce asset.* All things being equal, time is the most precious resource you have. My purpose is both to keep you from wasting time and to help you leverage the time you've got.

I am here to help you focus on great projects instead of ones that aren't going to serve you. You've got tons of ideas so I'm here to get you to the 1st profitable one. Then you can decide to grow that one to its limits or develop a 2nd profitable idea.

Example / How I Made a TV Show on a Zero Budget

My TV show was a fantastic learning experience. TV has some similarities to franchising. Successful shows can be leveraged into significant profits. And my story will show how this system can be applied to TV shows or even web TV today.

Developing this show was fascinating and in many ways the most entrepreneurial thing I did.

If you think about all the reasons *not* to create a network broadcast TV show it's almost overwhelming.

It would seem the deck is stacked against you because it looks like it requires:

- millions of dollars to shoot *even just a* pilot,

- relationships with network executives,

- broadcast experience, and

- everything else in between!

I didn't have *any* of those advantages and just happened to use this system by accident. I started off at level one by doing a little pilot on friends and favors.

I had some author friends as guests. One of my clients let us his boardroom and office on the weekends to use as our set (thanks, Marcus). I used an array of embarrassing home video cameras (also borrowed from friends) and I shot a 13-minute pilot. I did all the graphics stuff myself. Seriously! I just used what I had, right?

As luck would have it, serendipity smiled on me. I was coming back from Sydney with the pilot episode DVD in my hand. I heard on the radio that there was a new cable channel forming that needed new shows. I pulled over to the side of the road and placed the call. I was put straight through to the network executive, Mark. Mark said, "Don't wait, come in right now."

I didn't go home. I went straight to Mark's office.

While I was optimistic, I wasn't fooling myself with this pilot. I knew I didn't have a multi-million dollar studio piece here. It was just an idea at this stage. It was little more than a draft with minimal production quality. Mark put the DVD on and sat quietly. We watched it all the way through. The he turned to me and said, "Look, this is better than 97 percent of the rubbish I see come through here. Let's do a deal"

We signed an agreement right there. Amazing, right? I know I was shocked. And let me continue - there's more to the story.

I signed the show to cable broadcast, which is good. The holy grail of TV, however, is national broadcast. A year later, 20 episodes under my belt, I went on to have a conversation with the biggest network in Australia. It's the equivalent of Fox, CBS, ABC or NBC. I was talking to the chief programmer, Bryan, who decides what shows go on and what shows don't. I submitted a budget along with the best two minutes from season 1 as a trailer.

Remember, I was just one twenty-something guy in a little apartment in Sydney. I wasn't a huge production company. I was cutting this thing in my bedroom on my own PC. Seriously!

I remember talking to Bryan and he said, "Okay here's what it comes down to. We like yours but it's down to two. We like yours but you're not competitive price-wise. The other one, we can have much cheaper."

I said, "All right, who is it? Just tell me at least who I'm competing against." I thought he was going to tell me some local production company. Instead he said it was Warner Brothers out of Los Angeles.

Initially, I was crushed. I slumped in my chair, let out a huge sigh and thought, "Ohhh man, I'm in trouble here. How can I possibly compete some massive global conglomerate?"

Bryan said, "The truth is they've offered to give us the show free as a loss leader in our market to get themselves in." That means they were willing to give their show away for free, taking a huge loss, just to get into this new market. How could I match that?

I don't know to this day exactly what spurred my reply except the entrepreneurial spirit. I knew **what** I wanted but not the **how**. I said, "Great, what if I match their price?"

Bryan said, "If you match their price you got the deal."

I said, "Great, I'm matching their price."

He said, "Good," and 24 hours later I had a signed deal. There was, of course, the little problem of money; I had no way of paying for my season of a network broadcast television show. I was somehow going to make this show for zero dollars!

As an entrepreneur, there's nothing like a really solid **crunch** to help you find ways you've never thought of to accomplish your desired outcome. I raised a lot of money by getting good at sponsorship very, very quickly.

I had only a few months to raise the money and deliver the episodes. I ended up with 20 or 30 sponsors who funded the show for Channel 9. Everyone from Universal through Sony through toy companies like Funtastic helped me out. The show was a success. So, all I want to say is that, paraphrasing the Napoleon Hill Foundation's book 'Outwitting the Devil' - **failure is just a sign to get a new plan**.

Here are a couple key takeaways:

1. We're almost always our own worst critic, far more critical of our own work than other people are. If I didn't have the courage to talk about my idea even though I thought the thirteen-minute pilot was super basic none of this would have happened. **The key lesson for you is to view things as experiments and persevere.** You'll have to break out of the stories in your mind that say, "this won't work" or "nobody will like this idea."

2. Second, what's amazing is that I was able to work my way up from an idea to a cable show to a network broadcast show against all odds. And what did I do differently? **I got my head right.** And that's what this book is going to show you how to do.

Learn from My Failure

OK – so I've had some success. However, it wasn't always roses for me. There were tough times and hard lessons I had to learn, too. These were the kinds of lessons that can only be learned from failures.

Part of my upbringing and entrepreneurial mindset is being open to failure. I mean you have to be okay with failure to do real business experiments. In fact, you have to stop thinking about it as failure. It's just an experiment – some work and some don't. When they work – that's great. When they don't – make some changes and do a new experiment!

When you start new things and test new ideas failure is inevitable. Not every idea in its original form will succeed. In fact, many entrepreneurs become financially successful while succeeding only once out of every ten times. A major league baseball hitter gets paid at the top of his industry by failing seven out of ten times.

I've been very fortunate that none of my failures was a crushing blow. Nothing has ever made me outright stop. I've never gone bankrupt (the average millionaire goes bankrupt three times in life). But I'll tell you the story of one of my failures.

Example / Car Kids Torches 500 - My Big Fail

I had a stand out failure in the children's education industry. My business sold cassette tapes and CDs for children called _Car Kids_.

It was stories and games for children trapped riding in the car. The first series of cassettes tapes was a hit. We converted the first set of cassettes into CDs and they sold fantastically. Our second series did really well. The third one got us into bookstores.

That's when I got a call from a big independent bookstore near the beach in Manly which is close to Sydney Australia. The manager on the other end of the phone line sounded angry. He had 20 tapes and 20 CDs. He said, "I'm giving them all back!" I asked why.

He said, "Well, actually we had a customer come in and return a set because there's swearing. In a children's CD. Swearing!"

I said, "Swearing? That doesn't sound right. Let me look into it."

I went back and listened to it the whole way through. I couldn't believe it. Sure enough there was a point in this children's audio where a girl was lamenting her worst birthday ever. A parrot says to the little girl, "Bawk! This is your *crappiest* birthday ever."

The word 'crappiest' apparently was swearing. This was in the 1990s, not the 1950s or earlier. The word 'crap' was on regular TV at the time. But still some parents were offended and it would have reflected badly on the company to sell those copies. So we took the loss. In the 1990s, CD production wasn't as it is today where you spend $2.00 and basically you can have a jewel-case with full cover art shipped out from the warehouse. This was 20 years ago when it was way more costly per CD.

So, I had to take a whole run of 500 CDs and junk them. I ate the cost of the whole batch. We took out the word 'crappiest' and ran another batch. We played it for the manager and were back on the shelves at that high traffic bookstore. We learned an expensive lesson but didn't give up. We overcame and kept going. The lesson is to scale your experiments up from one copy. For us that error didn't come up until the third CD. Refine as you go. Iterate, iterate, iterate. I don't know if you can call it failure. It looks like learning to me.

Turning Failure into Success

To think I almost stopped after that third CD because of disappointment! I didn't have the perspective to know how good the sales numbers were.

The first CDs sold around 10,000 copies within Australia. When comparing equal market sizes that would be 150,000 copies in America. I was very upset because I thought I couldn't make a living selling only 10,000 copies. Little did I know, 10,000 copies was a massive success.

Had I stopped there, I'd never have known what I'd thrown away. I went on to sell the whole series to ABC. This sale made my next year's income in the span of one minute. The key issue for most entrepreneurs is it takes time, effort, smarts and these techniques. Even with all this good stuff it still requires you to apply yourself over time and figure out which pieces you love and which pieces you don't. You must figure which pieces work and which pieces don't. What's scalable and what isn't? You have to do a little failing along the way to get these answers.

To engage in this process the healthy and profitable way you must redefine failure. It's no longer *failure*. It's *learning*. You're one step closer to what does work. You can learn from my mistakes so you don't repeat them. But still you'll receive some undesirable feedback you'll have to learn from.

Napoleon Hill made a great point about this. I'm not really a Napoleon Hill guy and I still haven't read *Think and Grow Rich* from cover to cover. I'm sure I should.

What I have done is read one of the follow up books is called *Outwitting the Devil*. In this book Napoleon Hill describes failure as simply an indication to change direction and get a new plan. I'd go further and say *failure* means *refinement required*.

Many scientists believe failure equals feedback. Either of these two re-definitions of failure will keep your experiments in perspective. Most importantly, they'll keep you moving forward instead of getting discouraged.

So *don't* bet the farm. The 2 major themes of this system are:

(1) invest small sums of time and money, and

(2) get product to market quickly.

That's where your team comes in, since it's impossible to everything on your own. It's all about your core habits. Do you try to do everything yourself or do you delegate? Or *would* you delegate if you could but you don't have the team?! Read on, you're about to get all the answers.

Today, you've got to do things quick and light on your feet. This allows you to financially withstand the process and survive the refinement required until you get to something that brings in profits.

Why Learning Can't Replace Experience…and the Shortcut

Experience is by far the best teacher. I'm sure you're often heard the cliché 'Learn by doing'. It's a cliché because it's true!

That's the reason that I'm telling you so many stories from my past. It's so you can avoid my costly mistakes, learning from experiences I've already had. I'm trying to create a shortcut for you here! Even with all this, you'll still need to make your own mistakes and learn from your own experiences.

No one else can do this for you. You've got to make the commitment do it. When you sit in front of your computer, or sit on your couch and just dream, that's *not* experience. Even if you're working for a company doing internal tests, that's only partial experience. You can use that feedback to apply to your own projects. You've got to test your own projects and take the risks I've laid out in this system. Only when you risk your own cash and time will you gain true perspective and knowledge.

For example, if you write ten books but never release any of them, that's not experience. That's sitting in fear. Boldly releasing your product or service is the best way to overcome whatever is holding you back. What's the worst that could happen? **This system is designed to minimize your risk and cost as much as possible.**

How to Get the Most out of This Book

Who This Book is For

- Entrepreneurs

- CEOs and executives

- Home business and web business people

- Managers of product or service development

- Anyone who has an original idea and wants to get it out into the marketplace quickly and cheaply

Who This Book Isn't For

- People who want to stay in the old thought patterns

- People happy in their job and addicted to feeling 100% secure

- People scared to put their idea into the market

- People unwilling to invest a little time (3-4 hours per WEEK in the beginning)

- People unwilling to invest a little money (maybe a few hundred dollars to test most ideas)

My system doesn't break the bank, nor does it require you to risk your rent money, car payment, medical or home insurance. In fact, I insist you don't do that. Instead, this system requires you to invest some time. Or if you have more money than time, pay someone else to do the initial leg work.

Getting a Fast Start with This Material

The first thing I recommend is reading this book all the way through. These mind-bending ways of thinking about the world shift you out of old ways of thinking. You need a once over to take it all in, then start applying it.

I've worked with people at all levels of business. My most common client is a CEO of a substantial business. On average these people run a business doing around $20 million in sales per year. These are the people I work with day in and day out.

And here's the thing. When I share these methods and ways of thinking, these executives just sit there looking stunned. These are high-level business thinkers and they still don't know this stuff. That's why I'm suggesting that you should go through it once, then come back through and start implementing.

Just last week, I was in Atlanta working with a CEO. His company has been in business for 20 years. I started doing a makeover. I went over these tools and he got the wide-eyed look. I could see the light bulb come on almost like a cartoon character that has the little light bubble appear over their head. The CEO said to me, "Do you realize this changes everything?"

His entire business was now ready to leap forward, not just crawl. That's what updated business environment thinking and current technology can do for you as well. This system changes how you think about what you can do. It breaks you out of the cage the old way of thinking had you trapped in.

Example / 5 Minutes to Prototype

Let me give you an example from this week.

On Saturday I was talking with some friends about a new idea to create a steam punk ray gun product. On Monday I was with a client, an agency CEO – so I couldn't focus on the new idea - but I was already in action. I took five minutes before I began (we started our day at 8:45am) to drop an email. By 9am Tuesday (remember, I was busy on the Monday), I had found a new team member and had him working. By midday Tuesday I had a digital prototype.

It's now Wednesday. I'll have a prototype batch in production by close of business. It'll be in the market within a day of receipt.

And my current cost to market? Way less than $100.

Read that one more time. Total cost to market – less than $100. Sounds good, right?

The Meaning Of 'Entrepreneur'

The speed and minimal costs of this process just stuns the executives. So read everything through and get the ideas. Then understand what being an entrepreneur means. **To me, the word entrepreneur means experiment.** The most successful entrepreneurs like Bill Gates and Michael Dell didn't give up upon the first failure. They kept going. They got good at delegating and built the habit of focusing on growth.

Entrepreneurship is "the pursuit of opportunity without regard to resources currently controlled."

Imagine you're watching a scientist in her lab. She doesn't look like a nerd or scientist at all but clearly she's mixing stuff together in an experiment. One tube has red liquid, a second tube has green liquid, and a third tube holds blue liquid. She gets a quizzical almost maniacal look in her eyes, her blonde hair waves just a tad and a smirk creeps across her lips. She mixes the liquids together and then pooof! It explodes. The experiment fails. She pats herself down to check that her eyebrows haven't been burned off. Phew.

She gives herself a moment to feel the frustration, then shrugs it off and tries again with a different mixture. That's it! There's no emotional journey of hours, days or months! It's just a quick shrug and on we go.

She takes a notepad out and marks her observations. "Day 17, lead scientist's log, these 3 formulas didn't work. Formula 4 showed promise but wasn't quite right. Experimentation continues."

She thinks on it overnight letting her subconscious roam and search for the answer. She comes up with something new, keeps trying, keeps experimenting. She doesn't get emotionally attached to any one idea or experiment's outcome. Finally, the day comes where the mix does work. Eureka!

How to Define Your First Business Experiments

The trick is to define your business as a series of unemotional experiments. Does this work? Does that work? What does the market think? What will the market bear? Then you carry out these experiments in a step-by-step unemotional way, spending as little of your own time and money as possible.

Say you have a passion for art and you've been painting like crazy. That's not bad because at least you're active and producing. But what if the market doesn't want to buy that form of art? You've wasted a ton of time. What's preferred is to find the form of art people desire so much that they'll break out their wallets and buy. The idea is to conduct a series of experiment to find this out *before* you waste loads of time trying to create perfection. This way you know the art you spend time creating will sell.

Since we're not sure right out of the gate what kind of art they're going to go for, we've got to *ask* them. You can get some samples (or quick sketches of samples) into the market fast and see what people respond to. Do they like blue or green? Do they like pictures of puppies or pictures of people? The ones people ask or email you about are the ones you break out your canvas and create.

Treat this process as a low dollar scientific experiment. Don't break the bank testing your first idea. If testing with only a $20 budget is what's comfortable for you right now, then go with it. If you'd be happy to experiment with $50, $150 or $350 dollars, then that's fine too. Pick something that isn't threatening your rent/house payment or the car payment because if testing this idea threatens a house or car payment then all of a sudden you're emotional. And once you're emotional, you're in trouble. Emotion, in this case, can cause unwarranted attachment to a product or service form, slowing you down from finding the best refined form.

It's got to be a money investment where you're comfortable and happy. When you're happy your energy is good and you're thinking innovatively. It frees your mind to reveal the answers to you. If you're stressed, freaked out and unhappy, your best ideas aren't coming out of you.

If you'd like to know more about getting into an optimal state for innovation and creativity, check out my web site where I go into it in detail – http://www.timlevy.net.

Why This 1 Idea is Critical to Your Success

Once you've read all the way through, experiment with *just one* of your ideas. Use the tools you'll see in the following pages. The idea is to kick off a variety of experiments that have a comfortable scope, a comfortable budget and a comfortable timeframe. Then you just listen to what the market tells you. People vote with their wallets. Don't project what you want the market to tell you. If all you get back is silence, then that's an answer. Tweak or scrap the idea. If people contact you and want to buy but not in the form it's currently in, then adjust your idea to what they'll buy.

You'll be better at this the second time than the first, the third time than the second, and so on. You're not just testing an idea. You're getting good at building your team, delegating and forming profitable habits. You're flexing and building your entrepreneurial muscles. That's what being an entrepreneur is. It's a serial commitment. It's not, "I'm going to do this once, and I'll scream and curse the names of the authors because my very first idea didn't work", and then quit. It's about trying things out.

Use the very pointed mindset of a scientist. You must be vigilant against emotional attachments. You do this by keeping investment low and the perspective "It's just an experiment. I'm observing the feedback." Emotions lead to beliefs and once you've got a belief then you're attached. If the data comes back negative your mind finds a way to twist it to confirm your belief. You end up pursuing a bad project wasting tons of time and money.

Or worse yet, you get so upset you just give up. Let's not do that!

This is a way of approaching product and service development where you invest only the resources the idea has earned. While it's young, you put a little into it. As it brings in money you invest more in it. It's a merit based system that leverages online tools which simply didn't exist back in the day so things happen quickly and effectively.

As an entrepreneur or home business owner this is probably more leverage than you've ever had. If you're a CEO of a large company that makes $20 million or $50 million dollars per year then you've likely been using low leverage, expensive, old thinking. I'll lay out exactly what those old ways are and what the new ways are. This system has been refined in active big business primarily in North America, as well as Australia and elsewhere in the world. It's made a once difficult process easy, a once expensive process cheap, and a once slow development cycle lightning fast.

If you're working happily in a 9 to 5 job, with little time or money left over to test your business idea or product, the really nice thing about this technique is it's so light on its feet. It's quick and simple to do but you can actually take and leverage the small amount of time and money you do have to get something to market. When you find an idea that works you build it after hours and on weekends, hiring out more of the work as the profits come in.

You're now pursuing your passion, investing sums of money that any of us can afford, and solving your customers' problems at the same time. All the while, you're being conservative, using profits to scale the project instead of the risk of quitting your job cold turkey and hoping like crazy that your business idea works.

If you're in a career but looking to shift into a different industry this is a great transition tool. Imagine you're working for a Fortune 1000 company that does consumer products; dish soaps, detergent, etc. But your real passion is helping people solve their personal finance issues and prepare for their retirement. You're working 67 hours a week, but you've got a little more income from your job to invest. This system can work with almost none of your time invested, instead substituting a little more money to hire out the work.

This system lets you transition smoothly. It does so using the best and only proof that matters…sales. What's better proof and validation than when you're sleeping and someone you don't know opens up their wallet and buys? You know you've got something good when you wake up in the morning and there's money waiting for you. That's real leverage which leads to financial and life freedom…what this system is all about.

That's down the track a little way. I'm not suggesting you can jump in and have it overnight. But you can have that "first sale feeling". I love to get a little "you made a sale" text while I'm off doing something I love. For example, last week, I was in Hershey Indiana. I'm consulting with a great CEO, in the chocolate capital of America, and we're enjoying a fantastic lunch. It's me, the CEO and his wife, and a couple of other people. It's a beautiful lunch and ding! I get a text. Someone else bought something from me. The CEO can't believe I'm making money while we're eating.

This is the power of this system. I'd like to facilitate your transition to getting paid while you're eating lunch with friends or clients and banking cash while you're sleeping.

The Product that Proved This System

The
ENERGY
of
MONEY

From the best-selling author of *The Life Summit* and *The Entrepreneurial Toolkit*

TIM LEVY

The client work I do with CEOs made me realize how little people understand money. Even guys making big money don't understand how it flows and many would be in trouble if they lost their paycheck.

That's why I got this idea for a product to teach the mindset of how money works. I've had this mindset all my life because of the wealthy top-level business thinkers I've been around.

I settled on a name for the product…The Energy of Money.

How "4 Test Dummies" Revealed My Product Was a Winner

At the beginning of last year four or five clients all came to me suffering from a *lack of money*. I just assumed everyone knew what money was, how it worked, how it moved and therefore how one would go about getting it. I was stunned when I realized very few people saw what I believe is at the heart of the matter. Once I started teaching this mindset, the way I talk about it turned out to be tremendously helpful to a lot of people.

I started sharing this free of charge. I was taking my time working out the kinks in the system. I had to figure out the best way to explain it to people again and again. I got better and better.

It was slow developing because I hadn't yet mastered this "fast and cheap-to-market" system. I'm very results-oriented. That's one of my big hang ups. I can't stand it if things don't get a result in the real world. A conversation about strategy is very cute but means nothing unless it's implemented and successful. So for six or twelve months I worked with people to make sure the stuff in the "Energy of Money" product really delivered. At that point the product was at what I term <u>level one</u> (more on that in a moment).

I had one failure. I was working with someone using the "Energy of Money" process which also has an online component. He spent a little time learning and using the material. This particular individual, a client of mine, had implemented a bunch of stuff. He launched his idea into the market.

Around forty-eight hours later, he called me. He was so angry saying, "It hasn't worked!"

I said, "We only put it online a couple of days ago."

And he replied, "Yeah, but I'm not making money yet."

I said, "Well, we've only just started."

He thought this was some get rich quick scheme.

I said, "This is no snake-oil get-rich-quick product. It's very much the exact opposite of those. My system allows you to provide value to other humans in a way they feel compelled to compensate you for. If there's no energy, there's no money. Have you given great energy?"

He had not.

Still, I learned from this failure and it has become a strength. I now go to greater lengths to communicate to people they must be genuine, they must put energy and effort in to expect a result and it may not happen overnight. I communicated this better in the next version of "Energy of Money" product.

I worked it through the process and got past what I define as <u>level one</u>. You can work at this level very cheaply. You can do this with favors and friends from work, working the kinks out of the system, letting some first customers use it live in the market, and generate as much feedback as possible. I don't hurry these things. I much prefer to get it right, rather than trying to make a quick buck. There are lots of people online who write something, do little if any testing of the system, then they do these massive releases with 10,000 people buying it. I think "*How can you do that when you just wrote it! You don't even know if it works! You definitely don't know if there are problems in implementation or if people will struggle getting results.*"

The Energy of Money DVD Series

I then developed the "The Energy of Money" project into an online training course. Going from <u>level one</u> to <u>level two</u>, which is making at least $1,000 per month, took me 6 to 12 months. You don't have to move that slowly, but I prefer to do it right. I was still doing my normal daily work with clients during this 6 to 12 month period. My work developing "Energy of Money" was almost all done on afternoons and weekends. Once I was sure that the product was working well and I communicated it clearly, then I moved into production. I exceeded <u>level one</u> income the first day it launched. (I'll define all the product levels in the next section.)

I had a customer list growing during this process, because I had taken a long time at <u>level one</u>. I had a thousand or so people who already knew my work in other contexts. By January of last year the product was ready for prime-time so I mailed my customers about it. I had a stellar open rate of about 36%, and a buy rate of 16%.

The best way to find out if your product is viable is to test it on people you've never met who don't know you. You've been so close to the project you have tunnel vision. Often you make assumptions that people know all of the factors and all of the variables but they don't. So it takes a few product edits and updates to take everything out of your head and beam it into your customers' heads.

Taking the "Energy of Money" through this process from level one to level two over twelve months was an eye opener. It touched on level three the first day I launched it and goes there whenever I do a big push. Left without to its own devices, it sits happily at level two to this day. The "Energy of Money" proved this system and many of my clients are using this system successfully also. I've also run the Entrepreneurial Toolkit product through this process and it went much faster. I'm running a new product on innovation and creativity through this process as we speak.

Can I Do This?

If you have a business mind and access to the internet this system will work for you. You don't need a lot of capital. You don't need a ruthless personality. All you need is a few hours to read this book and put the top tools, tips and tricks to use.

The Core Concepts

What Are These Product Levels?

The product levels are a conceptual framework for getting your product or service into the market at an investment level commensurate with your income and feedback. What does this look like in real life? I like to think of products existing at three levels: <u>level one</u>, <u>level two</u> and <u>level three</u>. You move from one to the other by the process of bootstrapping. Let's have a look at those levels.

Level One

A level one product is pretty much just an idea and the simplest form of execution. You might call it a test piece or prototype. Since it's just an idea, I give it an incredibly small amount of my time. I spend a small amount of my effort and money on it. You create a best group of people to use this first version. They give you feedback to improve it in return for massively reduced pricing. After all, at this level *their feedback is more valuable to you than their cash!*

At <u>level one</u> your product or service is doing between **zero and $1,000 per month**. Once it goes beyond that, it's level two.

Level Two

A <u>level two</u> product has succeeded at <u>level one</u>. It's now doing between **$1,000 and $10,000 per month**. Once it exceeds $10,000 per month for three or four months, it's level three. You might take some of that profit and sew it back into the original product or service to create a higher quality level. You'll use all of the knowledge and feedback you've acquired in the market to refine your product or service in that way.

Level Three

A <u>level three</u> project has succeeded at <u>level two</u>. It's a much more polished version and it's going to be bringing in **over $10,000 a**

month. Of course you can grow higher from there. Again, you may choose to reinvest some or all of those profits until you have the best product you can possibly make, in consultation with constant iterative feedback from the market. It makes sense, right?

Here's When to Move Up a Level

I think of my products as **prototypes** when they're at <u>level one</u>. The resources that raise the products to level two are generally funded from the money I made from level one. As I mentioned, at <u>level two</u>, once I run the product up to $10,000 per month, I reinvest some of the profits to make a polished version, which moves the product up to <u>level three</u>. This means I'm never out of pocket. There's very little risk which is bootstrapping at its best. What if a <u>level one</u> project doesn't fly? Then I will either start again and head in a different direction or retire that idea to the virtual junkyard.

Example / The Story of How "Energy of Money" Moved Through the Levels

We're going to continue with how "The Energy of Money" grew and moved through these product levels. You already know the overview now here are the specifics.

Level One

When I launched my Energy of Money product, I did it first as a **prototype**. I used home-level equipment to make the videos, such as cameras and audio equipment I had in my office. I used a bit of my time to cut it. I outsourced a bit of editing too, just to give it that bit of a polish. For a couple of hundred dollars, I had a finished product. I'll tell you more about how to do that later.

Did I hawk it around the stores? No! I got it online inexpensively. I used PayPal as a merchant account because it costs nothing. There are no sign-up fees or monthly price with Paypal. I used a GoDaddy account to host the website. Since, I already had that account it cost me zero extra dollars. So, for virtually no cost, I got "the Energy of Money" online. I mailed it out to customers and straight away I made more than the thousand dollars I was aiming for. Waaay more.

That was easy, right? It was the perfect level one product. It was quick and inexpensive to get online, it did what it said on the box, and it earned money right away. It broke through the <u>level one</u> barrier quickly.

Did I settle for making more of the same product level? No! That's not what the product levels are about! "The Energy of Money" had proved itself in the limited marketplace, so I decided to go back and upgrade it to <u>level two</u> with some of my profits.

Now I felt better about spending more than just a few days on the product. It had proved itself at <u>level one</u>, so I was happy to spend a few weeks and some of the profits from <u>level one</u> to upgrade it to <u>level two</u>. That's what I mean by bootstrapping. I paid a couple of hundred dollars for <u>level one</u> and made quite a few thousand. I then took some of the profits from that and spent it on moving to <u>level two</u>. Do you see how this works?

Moving to Level Two

To make my new and improved <u>level two</u> product I went back and re-recorded some videos with better video and audio equipment. I hired a basic crew from Craigslist to help me at around $100 per day. Seriously.

Then, I added some new videos based on <u>level one</u> customer feedback. My beta group told me what was missing – so I fixed it!

In fact, I continue to improve it to this very day. At <u>level one</u> I sold the "Energy of Money" to about 50 different parties. After they got their programs they told me what was wrong with it, what needed to be fixed, what needed to be added, and what I'd missed. I had all this valuable feedback and advice to improve my product and it cost me nothing. These people paid for their product and they liked it well enough to tell me what they thought.

I made all those changes to move the product into <u>level two</u>.

They also gave me some great reviews which I could then use to leverage the product even further.

I redid all of the banking because the free Paypal account wasn't as suitable for the long term as a serious merchant account. Then I messed with the website, and tweaked that up to quality grade. I created a DVD and all the other stuff to make it a true <u>level two</u> product.

I also made an affiliate program. Then I went back on the market with the new and improved <u>level two</u> version.

<u>*What Happens Next?*</u>

The "Energy of Money" is currently living in <u>level two</u>. It brings in somewhere between a thousand and ten thousand dollars a month. Once it reaches a reliable ten thousand per month, I'll take it to <u>level three</u>.

Using some more time (because this program has proved itself twice over) I'll record it again. This time, I'll use a broadcast studio, with better equipment and a better quality than I can currently do in my own studio. It won't be just the same program with a bit of polish though. I'll take more examples and I'll expand the content. I'll use actual real life stories as a major part of the main content. How will I pay for that?

You guessed it. I'll use the proceeds from <u>level two</u>. The program is called the "Energy of Money," remember. It works both ways; for the customers and for me.

What I'm going for at this level is luxury quality. This is the McClaren F1 version (McClaren F1 is a $5.58 Million luxury supercar). <u>Level one</u> is about getting into the market quickly and cheaply. <u>Level two</u> is about proving longer-term viability. <u>Level three</u> is about going as far as you can to make the product the absolute best it can be. At least, *that's how I do it!*

The 3 Levels of Services

The three level approach doesn't just apply to products. It applies to services as well. Just think, you can get a service up and running for a couple hundred dollars. When it brings in the bigger dollars you can spend some of that on enhancing the service to the higher levels.

Here's how it works in another real-world example. (That's something you should know about me and the Entrepreneurial Toolkit. I give examples that have really happened to real people. This doesn't happen to perfect people in a perfect world. This happens to real people in the real world. That means you can make it work for you, too.)

Example / Tom's Career Change Journey to Coach

One of my clients (let's call him Tom) is just about to start a coaching guide.

I suggested that rather than starting from $5,000 a day, Tom might start at a lower price.

"In fact," I said, "Ask your market what price they'll pay."

"How does that work?" asked Tom.

"You can talk to people and ask, 'What would you be willing to pay for this kind of coaching?'" I said. "When you get a kind of consensus from a few people, you have your price."

"What if it's too low?" asked Tom. "I mean, dude, no one is going to suggest a high price, right?"

I took a moment to ignore the fact that he called me 'dude'.

"That's okay," I said. "When you get the price people are willing to pay, you can create coaching material to fit the price so you're making a profit and they're getting a good deal. You put that in as level one."

So, this is what Tom is going to do. He needs a phone and some leads. He can get the service online inexpensively at level one. Level one works with a phone call. It's going to be what I call a ninja approach. Ninjas don't lug around all the weapons and tools. They just carry the least needed to do the job. In business, they use the term 'minimum viable service' or 'minimum viable product'. That's what M.V.P. really stands for, right?! (Just a little sports joke, there).

Once Tom has his level one coaching service up and running, he can hold it there until it gets to a thousand dollars a month. When that happens, he comes back and makes improvements to get it to level two. This time, he'll want cards, letterhead, a website, a pitch book and all the other supporting material that I use.

If level one is a ninja with minimal tools, then level two is a little more Rambo. Remember Rambo? He goes into battle with every possible weapon from knife to pistol to shotgun to grenade to bazooka. Likewise, in level two you begin to straps on all the extras, using the money made in level one to finance it. Tom will expand the coaching material according to free feedback from his level one beta customers.

This is the bootstrapping model. It works for products and it works for services alike.

Further along in this book, we'll look at some useful websites. These are important. They help you get things done in <u>level one</u> and <u>level two</u>, for an incredibly small amount of money. You'll see how I've laid them out in order.

Some of them cost almost nothing; the price of a cup of coffee and less. Some of them cost a little more but as you move up the levels, you'll have profits in the bag to pay for higher quality.

Now, let's cover a couple more key concepts before we move on to the delegation technology itself.

How to Find the "Right" Price

One of the most important aspects of this system is pricing. Remember how I talked to Tom about that when he was setting the price for his coaching service?

A lot of people price their products and their services by making up a number. Seriously. They just make up a number that they'd like to charge. They just go to the market and say, "Well I do this or I can sell you this and it's going to cost you that. Give me an answer, yes or no."

The problem is if you do that, customers just think about whether they want that product or service at that price. They'll say "yes", or "no", but they won't give you any of the valuable free information we call *feedback*. "Yes" or "No" cuts off the dialogue before has had a chance to begin!

The Three Questions

I have a specific way I go about pricing my products and services. You can use it too. I ask **three specific questions** of the customer. These questions are easy, but they have a big effect on the customers. They seem to hand them the power in the partnership. People like power, right? In this case, it gives them the power to make an *informed decision*. That way they feel good about the decision they make, and they feel good about your product or service too.

I lay out the product or service I'm selling in a quick little pitch.

"I'm going to give you this coaching, okay? I have this kind of product... I'm going to give you this service... I'm going to polish your car, or cut your hair..."

Whatever it is, I lay it out briefly, simply and tell them just what I'm offering. Then I ask my first question.

The First Question

"At what price would this offer be a slam-dunk, no questions asked hot deal? At what price would it be **cheap** for the asking? What's that price?"

This gets people listening, because I'm asking their opinion. I'm putting them in the captain's chair. They like that, so they will give me a number straight off the top of their head. It's amazing how quickly and shrewdly people can price things. Then of course they look at me to see what I think of their price.

I show no emotion. As a scientist, I simply make notes, and then I ask my second question.

The Second Question

"Okay, so that's the price you snap up without thinking twice. So, what would be a **middle** price for this product or service? I mean, you might look at this new price and say, 'Hey it's good. I have to think about it though. I'll maybe check other websites, and have a look at the features to make sure it really fits my circumstances. It's a good fair price though, so when I've done my thinking and my checking I would probably come back and close the deal.'"

By now, people are getting the hang of this, so they come back to me straight away with a good, fair, middling price.

I make notes on that again and then I ask my third question.

The Third Question

"Okay, now I'd like to know what you'd consider **expensive** for this product or service. I want the price that you'd look at and say, 'Wow, that's expensive. This is a good product or service, but would I buy it? Can it be a good investment for me? I really have to think about it. Maybe I have to scrape some money to get this. I might talk to friends, and I'll definitely research online.'

Now, think of this as a kind of Apple price. Apple's never cheap, but it's always the best you can buy. In the end you'll probably buy it if you're the kind of person who goes for the quality product.

People come right back at me with the expensive, top-of-the-line, Apple-style price.

Profiting from this Pricing Information

Now, if I ask these three questions often enough, choosing people who might be the type to buy my product or service, I get a filled out statistical picture of what I might start to charge. This is the price that the market has dictated, not something I've simply made up because I want that amount of money. See the difference?

Now what do I do with the information? I might look at charging that middle price most of the time, but now and again I'll put the product on sale at the lower price. That will help me move some units or get some service work. Sales get a buzz going. People start talking about the product or the service and what a good deal they got.

The nice thing about this pricing is that it puts me in a position of power.

- If I want to sell more, I drop to the **low** price. If I want to move some quick units, get some great feedback or customer reviews I use the low price.

- If I want to make more money, I can position and build the value at the **middle** price.

- Once I'm up and going and overwhelmed by new business, I can put the brakes on a little by charging the **luxury** price.

However I set the price, *I'm* the one controlling the flow of money to my bank account.

The Specific Way to Get Fast Online Price Feedback

These days, there is a quick and simple way of asking these questions and getting the answers. These days you can do this quickly, easily and free using **social media**. If you actually do this process online on Facebook, Twitter or LinkedIn you can have ten or twenty people having this conversation. They'll bat it back and forth.

"What's this thing worth? What's dirt cheap, a fair price, a high price?"

If you follow the conversation you'll get opinions from five or ten people in a few minutes. The need for elaborate and expensive focus groups has almost entirely vanished, right?! Who needs them when you have a beta group on Facebook?! I love sneaky techniques like this.

The "Asking Live Audiences" Price Technique

It also works well when you're speaking live. I love speaking live. I have a few hundred people in the room, and I do my talk.

At the end I say, "I'm wondering if you'll help me do a quick experiment. I've got this new product," and then I'll hold up whatever it is.

"Right, this one is "Energy of Money". It comes in three DVDs and an online only version."

I give them time to digest this. Then I say, "Energy of Money" takes you through the conceptual underpinnings of what money is, how it moves, and how it works, because most people don't understand money flow. We change your mindset first, and then we show you exactly how to create what I call *money circuits* online. You can do this for yourself. You can change your job into doing something you love instead of doing what you feel you have to do."

Boom, that's the pitch. Now I want to ask my three questions; What would be cheap, what would be reasonable, and what would be top-dollar-hmmm-gotta-think-about-this?

If it's a live room, here's my technique. I say, "I'd like you to put up your hand if you feel this product is worth," and then I give them a high figure such as 500 dollars. No one puts up their hands. Next, I say, "How about 250? How about 100? Put up your hand if you would pay a hundred dollars for this and feel like it was good value."

At that point hands start to creep up, so I go on. "Okay how about 90, 70, 50..." and I keep counting down until I find that sweet spot where most people in the room have a hand up. That's my low price. When maybe half of the people have a hand up, that's my middle product price; the one I'll look to charge most of the time. That moment when the first hand goes up – that's my high price. Done!

OK. Let's move on to the team building and delegation <u>core material</u>.

Global Dynamic Team Magic

Over the last few years I've been working almost exclusively with the CEOs of substantial, often rapidly growing businesses. I began to see a common thread.

Each of these CEOs was a great team builder and delegator.

What I mean is that they never ever achieved success on their own. They always built up a team around them to achieve their business objectives. Simply put, you cannot be a one man band. You must build a team and delegate.

What I'm going to show you now is a new way to think of business and to build that critical team around you, even if you don't have a multi-million dollar budget to do it.

The New Way of Doing Business

The key concept here is what I call a Global Dynamic Team. I'll explain exactly how to build your own global dynamic team and why it's the best way to do business. Before I do, let's take a moment to learn from the past.

The Old Way = *The Hierarchical Model*

About fifteen years ago, I built a multimedia business from the ground up. I rented offices. I employed office managers, secretaries, people to answer the phone, designers, coders, and online people. Before you know it I had around 20 people on my full time payroll.

That was fine when I had clients coming in the door, but after a while, I found my job was basically just to keep business coming in to make sure all those people got paid! That's not why I started the business in the first place. This is the Hierarchical Model, because it depends on a hierarchy of a boss and employees, with the boss being responsible for paying the employees.

I sometimes refer to it as *bricks and mortar* thinking because it's tied to the idea that you need a physical office to run a business. That's dinosaur age thinking!

Most companies still use the Hierarchical model. To start a new product or new service and get into the market, you used to need a budget of at least a few hundreds of thousands of dollars. You'd rent or get a small office space. Maybe do elaborate and expensive marketing campaigns, invest and develop a business plan, spend a long time developing the product and most importantly hire staff. You'd hire full-time people to bring our amazing idea into the real world. Every time you hire a staff member they cost double or triple their salary because of overhead. Remember, you have to pay their salary, employment taxes, their computer, their phone, their desk, their office space, their 401K, their insurance, and many other costs.

If you pay this staff member $50 an hour, you'd have to multiply that $50 per hour by as much as three to earn back the overhead and eke out a profit. These are the dreary numbers operating under the old Hierarchical model.

Every time you want to employ a new staff member you're risking $30, $50 or $80 thousand dollars per year before one dime of profit. So you're taking all sorts of risk to develop a team, to develop a product or service and then get it into the market. You're risking all this and you don't even know if people will buy! No wonder so many of these businesses and startups go belly up.

I was working with one of these businesses last week. It's an agency that's been in business for over 25 years. What they would do is build their business by chunks of $300,000 because that covered $100,000 in salary, $100,000 in overhead and then there was $100,000 leftover as profit. So they needed $300,000 worth of new business to get $100,000 more profit. It takes a lot to grow the business using this model and it's risky.

Most CEOs I run into when I speak all around the country and sometimes abroad, upwards of 90%, 95% easily, of the CEOs still think and work this way. And it feels like the bigger and older the business is, the more entrenched this old way of thinking has become.

These CEOs run $20 and $50+ million businesses. They've been growing slowly. I'm talking six months, twelve months or longer just to get to product version 1.0. You don't need to do that anymore.

The new Global Dynamic Team model is much better, less risky and faster.

The New Way = The Global Dynamic Team

Let's think about how a Hollywood movie is made. It begins when the producer comes up with an idea for a movie and hires a writer.

- Does that producer immediately start hiring the actors?

- Does she hire the camera crew and the scouts and the caterers?

- Does she have all those people waiting doing nothing while the writer is writing the script?

No way. The writer works completely on their own until the script is finished. Their job is done. They get paid. They get 'fired' from this job when their work is done and they move on to their next gig.

Next, the script is pitched to a studio and a director. Do we hire the hire actors, crew and marketing people yet? No way. You **only hire people on a needs basis**. People are only there when they're needed and then they're gone.

It's the freelance model. Television shows are also done this way. People are hired for the shooting season. Once the shooting's done, the film crew and actors leave. Now it's editors who are employed. Once the editors are done, there might be only a producer and someone to deliver the finished episodes to the network. You've met him, he's the guy on the bike!

The idea in the Hollywood Model is to expand and shrink the workforce **dynamically** based on the work that's in front of you.

This Hollywood model lends itself to the Internet age fantastically well.

When you put the two together, the Hollywood model + current technology, you get the new model I call the Global Dynamic Team model.

These days it's possible to hire people quickly. You don't have to hire people full time. Of course, you *can* still have full time employees, if you find they're doing so much work for you they're virtually working full time anyway. And full time is great if you need them in the office every day, to hang out with you.

But I find nine out of ten people I work with I don't need in that context. Whenever they can work virtually this is a good way to go. It keeps my office overhead down, and makes insurance, 401k and such things dwindle to *almost nothing*.

These days, I get most of the work done for my business via a web site called Elance. It's one of the world's largest **global databases** of freelance workers. And they're so keen to work with me!

In other words, I use freelancers to do most things. Don't worry if you've never heard of Elance - that will be explained later. The key idea here is that **I just employ people for the exact duration I need and not one second more.** When the project is finished, I don't have to terminate their employment.

It just naturally ends when their part of the project is done!

And here is the even more interesting thing; I have them compete for the jobs, so they name their own price. I usually get to pick out of ten or twenty options. I pick the price I like, the person I like, with the experience I like and get that task done.

I get to expand and shrink my global freelance workforce for optimum efficiency.

When I want a logo designed, I get it done then that contract is over. When I want a website created, I get it done by accessing my global workforce, then it's over. When I want some text transcribed, I get it done without any overhead. I don't really care if the person is in North America, India or Peru – as long as the work is done well!

I used to try, as an Australian, to hire Aussies and Kiwis. I was also partial to Americans, Canadians and Brits. Then again, maybe that's racist in this day and age – so now I hire try to hire based on merits instead of location!

Some jobs happen more frequently, so I get them done by the hour. I mean you won't hire a bookkeeper full time, because you need only a few hours of a bookkeeper's time a month. It works for the bookkeepers too, because they can work for other people on other days.

Of course I find great people as I go, so I wind up working with them over and over. Those people become part of my as-needed team. I have around thirty people I work with repeatedly and it's always expanding.

How You can Access Quick, Cheap and Global from Your Chair

What's happened now is stunning. Technology has fueled the Global Dynamic Team model. Instead of having access only to the people who live near you or within a reasonable commute, you can reach anyone in the world through instant online freelance communities.

You can have these eager workers do tasks for as little 10 cents. Seriously. I'm not making this up. 10 cents.

Now I'm not saying they're going to edit a video for 10 cents. That's not fair. But you can have micro tasks done for as little as 10-20 cents, and larger more involved tasks at $10.00 -$20.00 per hour. There's an amazing quality level at this pricing. I work with a terrific designer out of the UK who lays out an entire 60 page book for approximately $30.00 per book. I work with editors who do a task that used to cost me $5,000 to $10,000 down to a tenth of that.

So it's a combination of this new global thinking, online technology and access to skilled people all over the world. The ease of working virtually has evolved to where you can get international people working on your behalf. The natural forces of competition have done the rest, bringing prices down to what the market will pay.

There's amazing opportunity to take what has been an expensive or glacial paced process and instead sprint into the market with little cash out of pocket.

If I have a six step process, I just kick it off to the first member of my team. My team does all the steps passing work from one to the next until the final product comes to me for quality control. I add my special passion, experience and value before I send it out to clients. I've got this down to a science based on my own experiences in television and my internet and technology passion.

Try to realize the magnitude of this. From your desktop you can gather a global team of skilled workers. I have a team of around 30 people I'm working with almost every week and my cost is fractional to the old hierarchical, bricks and mortar way. I mean not even a tenth, more like a 20th or 50th of the old way cost. Even better, I get things done lightning fast without the fixed overhead management cost.

Technology has improved other business areas. The marketing you needed before was cost-prohibitive. To run a magazine ad you were making at least a decision of multiple hundreds of dollars and quite often multiple thousands of dollars. That's just to run one ad to see if it works. That's lots of financial risk.

Now you can get on Google and only pay for results. You pay each time somebody clicks your ad. Your ads could be live within two to three hours or within one business day. The magazine ad won't be producing for you for several months. With internet ads you're making a 10 cent decision or $5.00-$10.00 decision. Then you refine your campaign based on how it performs. It's closer to instant feedback, risking way less of your disposable income. You're comparing $10.00 or $100 experiments instead of $1,000 or $10,000 experiments or more the old way.

You can get your idea made, marketed and figure out whether it has legs in a few days. Since it costs less and you know much faster whether it's a winner you get to test more ideas. This speed and low cost is the beauty of the Global Dynamic Team style delegation.

Once you find a winner you can grow that idea through all available means using the profits.

I'm not saying you won't ever use traditional forms of media because magazines have extraordinary reach with a focused on-topic audience. Radio and television still work because of their extraordinary range. But before you risk big money you knock the kinks out of your marketing communications, you polish your product/service from version 1.0-2.0-3.0 and when your communications and product is ready for primetime you roll it out big.

The 1/10 Cost System Explained

With this new technology people are learning to work differently. People used to think of work as only two paths. A part time job was the smallest unit of work you could do, right? You could get a job, either full-time, or part-time. Most companies hired full-time (and still do). It's just how they think! There's still full-time work and probably always will be.

Now, simply put, there are more options.

Therefore, the smallest commitment I can make is no longer a five days a week, forty hour unit of work. Now a specific skill may cost $6.44 an hour but instead of having to buy that skill 40 hours a week, 50 weeks a year, I can now buy that same skill one, two or five hours as needed. This person is now free to accept 50 jobs, 100 jobs at the same time. This person is free to leverage their workday way better than they ever could before. It's lower risk because they don't have to worry about only one boss who might run low on money and can't make payroll this week. It's a strategy of risk diversification that matches our times.

This new system is fantastic for the entrepreneur and the ambitious worker. It comes down to that micro level. It's super efficient. People get creative to make it work. For example, I know some people transcribe by running the audio through software. They check over what the software spits out and make their quick cash. They might be earning that $5.00-$10.00 in moments because of their savvy. I say more power to them.

As long as I get the outcome I want this is opportunity on both sides. It creates more global opportunity. It makes the world more abundant which is good for all of us. Now as an entrepreneur you can find the best source to get the work done cheaply and quickly.

How to Build your Global Dynamic Team

For me, the days of the Hierarchy Model are gone. With this system you look at the level your project is at and then apply a commensurate amount of time and energy.

In those early levels I'm using freelancers. I'm expanding and shrinking my workforce literally by the hour to get those small jobs done. I want them working hard and fast to get that prototype into the market quickly.

Next, we'll go through the 3 main sites in order of task size. I'll give some examples of specific tasks that make sense for each website so you'll go in knowing exactly what tasks to post to which site. For

MTurk.com you're talking about the smallest tasks, some of which you can get done for only 10 cents each. For the next larger and more time consuming batch of tasks you'll go to the Fiverr.com marketplace. For the highest level skills and time intensive tasks you'll go to Elance.com.

For Small Jobs Use – MTurk.com

MTurk.com is a very cool marketplace to get very simple tasks done. You can get tasks done for as little as 10 cents. You can specify how many units of a task you want done. MTurk is owned by Amazon.com so your info is secure.

I haven't used the site much. My business partner Clint has paid for tons of work here. He'll tell you his experiences in this section.

Hey, Clint Evans here. I've paid for lots of mini-blurb writing tasks through MTurk.com. If you understand anything about websites you know there's a need for new material on your own website as well as publishing blurbs and interesting articles to other websites to get exposure and links coming into your website.

MTurk is great for getting 100 to 150 word blurbs written. I don't do this much anymore for links. Now it's best to get 4 or 5 initial comments on your articles. This way people see your site is a happening place.

Imagine 2 restaurants. One has only a couple empty spots in the parking lot. The 2nd one across the street has 1 lonely car in its parking lot. There's no line at the first but it's almost full. Which one do you choose?

If you're like most people (and not an adventurous weirdo like I sometimes choose to be) you go to the restaurant with lots of people. You assume the food there must taste better because everybody's eating there. So obviously, if everybody chose it, it must taste better and be higher quality.

People project this belief onto websites. If they're looking around your site and nobody's commenting or interacting it's like the 'ghost town' restaurant. So paying for 4 to 5 initial comments is like cars in your website's parking lot. It tells people your site is the happening place and they better jump in. MTurk is an uber cheap place to buy these first 4 comments. I pay around 25 cents to 50 cents for a 100% unique, on-topic comment. So 5 comments would be at most $2.50.

Other tasks which are an excellent fit at MTurk are: getting Facebook likes to your site's articles (again I'd buy 5 or 6 likes to get your counter off of 'zero' and start the ball rolling), 8 or 10 Tweets for your article, 5 or 6 Google +1's, and 5 to 10 repins (assuming you have a photo in the article, which you should, this will help your presence on the uber popular Pinterest.com website).

Again, this helps your social popularity. It encourages your readers and visitors to participate because 'everybody's already doing it'. You become the popular kid hosting the party everyone wants to be at. If you're concerned about buying the first few, don't be. It's like the bartenders who put the first 5 or 6 one dollar bills (and usually one $10 bill) in the tip jar. This tells the patrons people have already tipped so they should also.

MTurk tells you what jobs are good for them when you go to the 'create' tab inside your account. So first, you sign up for a free account. On the right side of your screen is the *Get Results from Mechanical Turk workers* section. Click the 'Get Started' button.

Once you've followed the wizard, setup your account, and funded it you're ready to rock. Funding is easy because your payment info is already stored in your Amazon account. Now, it's time to post your first task request. Inside your requester account click on the 'create' tab. It's second from the left to the right of the 'home' tab. Click 'new project'. On the left it shows you what categories of projects people hire on MTurk. I use 'writing' and 'other' the most. Follow the wizard and create your task.

Reward per assignment is how much you'll pay for each entry. Beware, if you offer too little nobody will do the assignment. Number of assignments per HIT for our example would be 5 because you're looking for 5 blog comments. Time allotted per assignment means how long each worker has to complete the assignment once they've accepted it. For a blog comment I'd give them 1 hour. HIT expires in is the deadline. I do 7 days. "Results are automatically approved in" option tells workers when they'll get paid (if you accept their work). I do 3 days so they know they'll get paid quick (or they'll know if I rejected their work and have a chance to improve it for acceptance).

Click the 'Advanced' link in the lower right. Click 'Worker requirements' link. Then you can choose the options of which MTurk workers get to see your task posting. You can set the quality level of worker who sees your post. This saves you time because low quality workers won't see your posting. Therefore, you get fewer junk entries. Once you've chosen these options click the 'design layout' button.

This is your title and description screen. Be specific but not lengthy in your task description.

Here's an example posting. You can follow this format when posting your small tasks to MTurk.

Example – MTurk Task Description Sample

[

Title:

Short, Sweet, Easy Writing --> Quick 100 word comment!!

Description:

Write A Comment to an Article (110 words) --> WRITING MUST BE 100% UNIQUE. I Check and if you copy from other sources you won't get paid. This is very easy to do so it's not worth taking a shortcut.

The purpose of this task is for you to write your response to a page on my website as if you were a reader interested in the topic. You're joining in the conversation or asking a question. You can address me directly (ie: "Clint your article missed the mark." Or "Clint I liked this specific part of the article…")

You'll be given 2 pieces of information: 1) a URL to visit, and 2) a keyword phrase to use in your comment.

1) URL = http://www.popularmoviedownloads.

com/a-surefire-way-to-download-movies-to-zune-successfully

http://advice4unow.com/internetmarketingnews/download-movies-legally

http://spraybooth.org/entertainment/simple-way-to-download-movies-from-internet.html

2) KEYWORD PHRASE = Download Movies
Guidelines to follow for the comment

   * Your comment must not have grammar or spelling mistakes (US English please).
   * Your comment should be written in first person, in a casual conversational manner.
         o An example would be: "I was checking out INSERT KEYWORD and found this article..."
   * Your article can be either a positive reaction to the page URL, a neutral response, or constructive critique. Negative comments without constructive criticism will be rejected.

   * Creativity, humor and imagination are encouraged.
   * Your comment should be 110 words or

more. *** IMPORTANT - less than 110 words is the number one reason for rejection.

  * Your comment must contain the KEYWORD PHRASE exactly as it is. This phrase must not be at the very beginning or very end of the your comment.
  * Do not use the URL in the comment
  * Comment should be family friendly language (no swearing or «bad» words).

  * No sentences or phrases longer than 3 or 4 words should be copied directly from the original article (or anywhere else on the web).
  * If you want to make a short quote from the original article (maximum one sentence), you can include it inside "quotes the way this phrase is".

]

That's it for the description. Tell them what you're looking for and what's unacceptable. You'll still get a few garbage entries you have to deny. That's cool because MTurk.com allows you to accept or reject. Obviously, you don't pay for the entries you reject. Don't be too picky though. Remember, these are super cheap tasks. Operate in good faith and keep MTurk.com the vibrant community it is so everyone benefits from it.

MTurk.com is very easy to use and handy. I encourage you to get in there, experiment, and see your project blossom. Now back to Tim to cover Fiverr.com and Elance.com.

For Medium Jobs Use – Fiverr.com

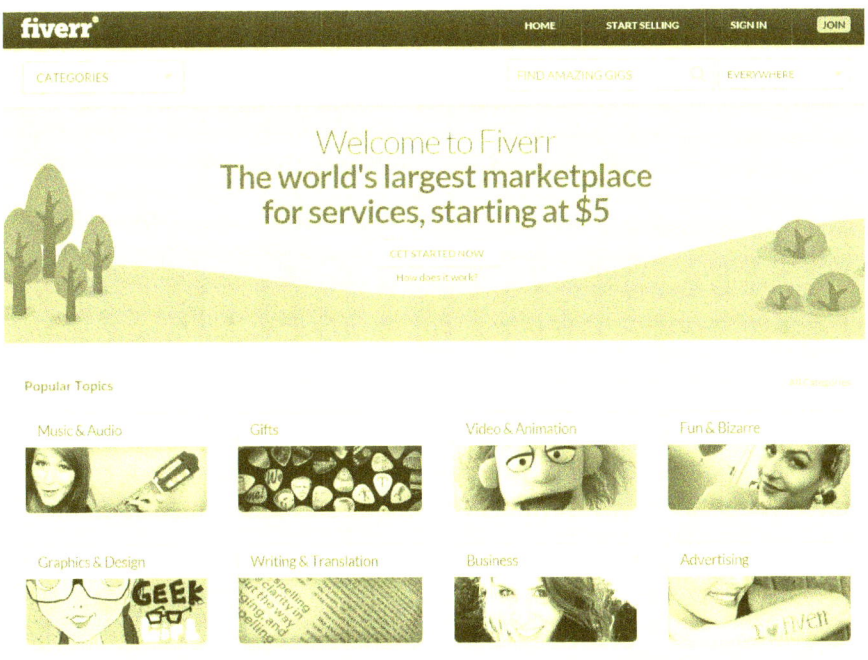

Fiverr.com is a freelance web site where people do "gigs" as they call jobs and services, for a $5.00 fee. Simple, right?! It's the world's largest data base of things people will do for $5.00.

When I first introduce this idea invariably people say, "What could possibly get done for $5.00. Surely nothing I want in my personal or business life could ever be done for $5.00." This belief is false. In fact, Fiverr.com itself is expensive when you compare it to sites like Mechanical Turk (MTurk.com).

The first thing for you to know is $5.00 buys you a lot, depending on where you are. For example, if you're living in downtown New York with high prices then $5.00 doesn't buy you much. But if you're living in Austin you can buy more for a $5.00 bill because the cost of living is much lower. Mississippi is lower than Austin and outside of America, somewhere like the Philippines, $5.00 U.S. buys you even more. So, it's important to understand that Fiverr is just a market place for people to come together. One person says, "I'm happy to do this for five bucks." When a second person says "I'll give you five bucks if you do that for me," then you have an agreement.

So that's the first thing about Fiverr. You must adjust your beliefs. You can get very useful things done for only $5.00.

Most people laugh when they first go to Fiverr's front page. The gigs on the front page are usually like something out of a bad comedy.

It's full of stuff that you'd probably never get done.

Here are some funny examples –

- $5 to get a video of a fat man singing you happy birthday wearing nothing but a thong. Not helpful except as a prank.

- $5 to have a hot girl pretend to be your girlfriend on Facebook for a day. Not helpful.

- $5 to get a cartoon of yourself looking 'hideously ugly'. Not helpful.

- $5 to send you a crochet key chain. Not helpful for most businesses, although maybe a nice gift!

What's interesting is as you scroll down you start finding staggeringly helpful things people will do for only $5.00.

Here are helpful examples –

- $5 to design a logo for your new product or service. Very helpful.

- $5 to create a wordpress install for your new product or service. Very helpful.

- $5 to transcribe and edit 15 minutes of audio (maybe the copy for your web site) into a word document. Very helpful.

- $5 to get a video review of your product or service to use on your site as a testimonial. Very helpful. Just be clear you want an unbiased review.

- $5 to get your new copy posted to your wordpress site with perfect on-page SEO. Very helpful.

Do you begin to see how this works?

Follow My Lead - How I Use Fiverr

Let's go through a couple examples of how I use Fiverr all the time. I've bought hundreds of Fiverr gigs. One gig I buy all the time is what I call a <u>level one</u> logo. It doesn't have to be perfect. It just has to be a quick logo I can use at <u>level one</u>. Then I go back and spend a little bit more time and money to upgrade the logo once the project proves profitable.

Type the search term "logo design" into Fiverr now. When I do this today there are 9,212 people who would like to design me some kind of a logo. They have samples so I can take a look at their styles and then pick one. $5.00 and bam, a couple days later or a couple hours later in some cases I've got a new logo for my new entrepreneurial idea.

Let's say I want to make that logo into a business card. I just type "business card" into Fiverr and there are 2,494 people who would do a business card for me. I have them use the logo I just got designed.

How about a little bit of logo animation? I want to use 30 seconds worth of an opening title for a YouTube video I'm going to do on my new concept. There are 1,578 people willing to do that for me.

I love to write but I'm a little slow, so I tend to do things by speaking. I record that audio and then have it transcribed. If I typed in "audio to transcribe", 1500 people want to transcribe my audio for me $5.00 at a time. 582 are glad to edit my new transcription document.

What about a press release? There are 10,905 people who want to write me a press release. So there are extraordinary things you can get done for $5.00.

My Step by Step Fiverr Process

The next thing to know about Fiverr is how the process works. It's very safe which is why I love it. Five bucks is low risk so if I lost it, I wouldn't be too upset, right?

Even so, I don't want to buy a gig by giving the other person my credit card details or personal information. Then I could be open for identity theft. It's important to me that this whole thing is safe. All my contact info is kept by Fiverr itself so the gig providers and buyers never see each other's personal info. Most people don't even give Fiverr their credit card details because you can just use Paypal to pay. This provides an extra layer of security.

You create a free Fiverr account, sign in and then you look up whatever gig you want. Hit buy and it goes to PayPal. PayPal sends $5.00 from your account over to Fiverr. Fiverr never sees your credit card info this way.

Fiverr then holds my $5.00 in escrow. It doesn't give it to the person that's doing my gig until I say the gig is complete. I have a dialogue with the worker I hired through a special screen to communicate back and forth until I get my end result. A couple days later it comes back to me and says "delivered".

Many Fiverr providers are extremely hungry for positive reviews, so in most cases they go above and beyond to make sure I'm happy. If I need a couple of drafts for this and that, it doesn't seem to be a problem. Once I hit the thumbs up button saying the gig is complete and I'm happy, Fiverr releases the money. The provider gets the money and the review. I've never been at risk at any point in the process.

Keeping your financial details secure is really important when you're transacting with a random person. They could be from Russia, America or Australia and be tempted or actively looking to steal your identity. These protections allow you to use the site and they keep everybody honest.

How to Choose Which Gig to Hire

Every Fiverr gig shows lots of information before you make a transaction. There's a little flag to tell you where they are in the world, their past reviews, details of what's included in their gig, a gig rating, and estimated delivery time. So there's a lot of information to help you make a good decision. I often use this information to help people outsource pieces of their own job, specifically the pieces they're not loving.

They build their own little teams to handle job duties they dislike. This makes their life quicker and they perform better.

"For everything you love to do, do it. For everything else, delegate!" Tim Levy.

Something else I do and recommend you do as well is commission multiple gigs at the same time because it's only $5.00 each. You have a higher chance of getting what you want from three or four people instead of "betting the farm" on just one. For example I had character design done for one of my children's books. I hired four designers, working at the same time because I figured I might not like one or two of them. I wanted to stack the deck in my favor and get the four designs back sooner rather than hiring them one at a time. So I spent $20.00 and felt much better about getting a result I'm satisfied with fast. Once you find somebody who's good for a particular task you can just hire them for $5.00 to handle that for you in the future. There's no need to multi-commission duplicate gigs.

I'll take you through what I do when I want a task done that I've never had done before. I get artwork done all the time. I'm talking cartoon characters from scratch. If I had never gotten an artwork Fiverred then I'd just go to Fiverr.com and type "character design" in the search box (without the quotes around it). It comes up with 381 matches.

Fiverr sorts by what they call '**auto**' which is kind of random. I like to change the sorting to what they call '**rating**'. This sorts the best, most active people first. Straightaway I'm putting gigs in a more helpful order to save me time. If you need the gig completed ASAP, you can sort it by what they call '**express gigs**'. The provider delivers these gigs within 24 hours. Or '**new**' if you want the most recently created gigs. Usually these are new people, unproved and they won't have ratings on the gig. So I sort by '**rating**'.

I have a little look at the flags. When it comes to character cartoons, I love the anime style, so I look for the Japanese because that's the home of amazing anime. That's probably just my own bias and I'm sure there are Westerners who are very good at drawing anime characters. Look down the left hand column at the images to see the person's artwork. If what I see looks terrific, I open up their gig.

I right click and say *open link in new tab* so I can have three or four gigs open at once. I can compare them more easily. The gig page tells me how many positive and negative reviews. This is close to the number of times they've done the gig because almost every buyer leaves an honest review after the gig is delivered. This gig I'm looking at has 72 positive reviews and zero negative reviews. If you have 72 reviews and everyone said that it's great, it's probably great. And this particular person has lots of samples which is further proof. It builds my confidence their style matches what I want and they'll probably deliver me a good result.

Fiverr is a wonderful collection of skilled people willing to do tasks for only $5.00. You'd be surprised what you can get done for five bucks. Go to the site and hire three or four gigs. It's worth twenty bucks just to familiarize yourself with the system. There's virtually no risk and everything to gain.

For Large Jobs Use – Elance.com

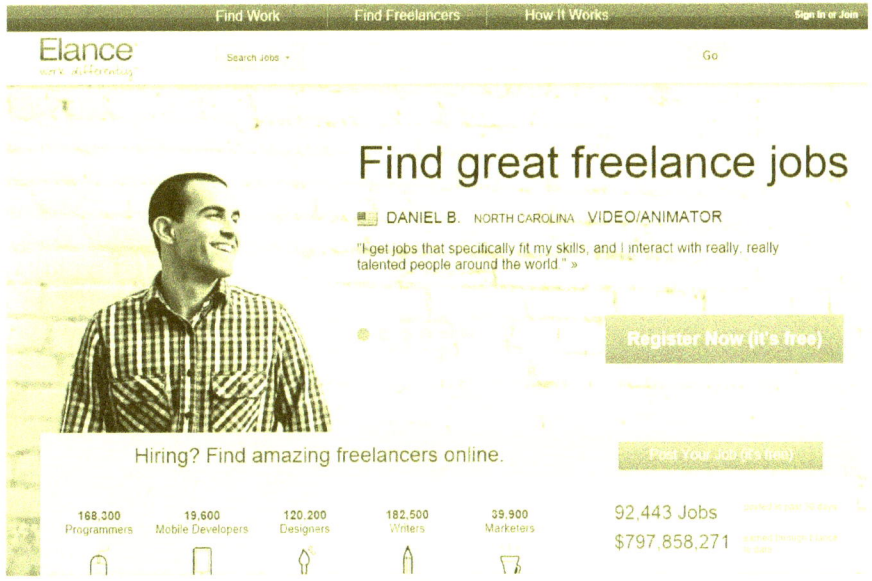

I've explained why the Elance way of doing business (the Global Dynamic Team model) is such a good fit for the current working environment. It reduces overhead like crazy. But what *is* Elance?

Elance is the best place I know to find freelancers from all over the world, ready and willing to do a huge a variety of tasks. I use it project by project. If I need something designed, I get it designed by an Elance freelancer. If I need a web site made, I hire an Elance freelancer. If I need a 3D model made, I hire an Elance freelancer. Are you getting the picture?

I **never** hire a designer or a web person for my business on a permanent basis. This keeps my overhead low and it allows me to access professionals across the world in different fields. I wouldn't get this access if I had them all working for me in any context at my office. So let's jump in now and see how it looks.

Welcome to all my tips and tricks about how to hire people, what to look for, and how the process works for Elance.com.

Elance.com is not the only freelance site. There are various competitors, including Odesk, but Elance is the one I started with and perhaps it's the world's largest database of freelancers. You could really get anything done on Elance.com, especially jobs that are too big for Fiverrr.com.

Follow My Lead - How I Use ELance

I've hired lots of Elance freelancers. I've hired jobs including: editing books, creative design, web development, online research for business leads, and bookkeeping. It's an incredibly diverse group of people. Have a look at elance.com to see what's happening. When I looked today, I found over 100,000 separate jobs had been posted over the past month, and over $700,000,000 has been made. Yes, that's $700 Million in business. Just browse different sorts of things you can get done here in marketing, consulting, finance, design, and programming.

My Step by Step Elance Process

The first thing to do is to get a free account. This goes for whether you want to do some work here and get paid or whether you want to get some work done. So get yourself registered. When you're registered, sign in.

When I sign myself in, there may be a security question here just to make sure I am who I say I am.

Here are some examples of the work I have going right now –

- A transcript and edit of a new book project

- A 3D model for production of a new product project

- The design and layout of a client blueprint project

- The SEO of a web site

- The traffic / pay per click campaign for a web site

- A research project for cruise ship speaking

- A promotional animated video is in production

- All of my accounts, invoicing and book-keeping

So you can see there's a wide variety here.

How to Setup an Elance Job Posting

So how do you find someone to work for you? Well, in Elance jargon, you need to *post a job.*

How do you post a job? Well you go and click a button called '*post your job*' and it's incredibly simple. For example, I'd like to get some articles written. I'm looking for articles based on content I already have on my website. Then they'll post these articles to different places on the web who accept written articles.

I put *article marketing* as the job and then I describe it. When doing a description I suggest you keep it brief but give it plenty of thought.

When I write a job ad I highlight the experience I'm looking for or possibly an experience in a certain genre. Maybe you're looking for an editor who specializes in children's books. Or a lawyer who focuses on estate planning or forming new businesses.

I emphasize three things in my Elance ads:

1)   Talent

2)   Experience

3)   Culture

I might write something like this.

"Hello, I need to have someone write up a series of articles based on existing content on my website.

I can give you all the URLs. Some of the material is already in text form, some is in video form and so on. I'd like you to write the articles, then post them to appropriate directories online.

I'd like to order maybe ten articles at a
time. It would be extra handy if you had
experience in the self-help and business
niches-because that's what I do! Looking
forward to being in touch."

That's a nice casual job ad. I think it's important to write these ads with your own style because that way people who like your style are drawn to you.

Let's look at some of the other things we need to specify.

Category of work. This one would go in sales and marketing. The sub category might be email marketing. All the categories and sub categories are listed, so you just click on the ones that are suitable and follow the prompts.

Next, I have to decide whether I want a fixed price. I decide I do. My budget is going to be less than $500.00 and the great thing here is that allows other people to tell me what they think this job is worth. I don't set the price, they set the price and I get to choose the price that suits me best.

As to the further options, the one I like here is the preferred location. I get to choose someone from the region where I'm doing business. Anyone's welcome to apply but I'm looking for people in North America, for example. I want to post this job for maybe seven days.

Next, there's the privacy option. I can put the ad where everyone can see it and then I'll get lots of applications, but if I choose private, then only the people I invite to look at the application can see it.

There are still other options. If I wanted to pay extra, I could get my job featured. I haven't used the featured option because I get plenty of replies so don't see the need to spend the extra cash on it. If I don't want that, I hit '*No thanks*'. Then I double-check everything and when it looks right, I hit '*Post*' and the job is online.

What's amazing is that this job now goes out to everybody who's searching for work. If the job is up for seven days, I might come back to look tomorrow or I might wait until the listing closes. Then I look at the proposals job seekers have sent me. There will be a whole bunch. I scroll down and pick the ones that seem suitable for closer examination.

Example / Hiring A Global Dynamic Team Bookkeeper

I'm going to give you an example for my Australian bookkeeper job. I had quite a few offers and some were terrific. Some I declined straight away because they weren't in Australia. I really wanted someone who knew the Australian system so even though some of the hourly rates in India and some other places were down at $5 or $7 an hour, I wanted to pay a little extra for someone in Australia.

That way I knew the bookkeeping would be done right for Australian conditions. I looked closely at all the ones who specified they were in Australia.

To break down the selection process, I looked at the ratings from past clients. The person I actually selected, Amanda, had a rating of 4.9 out of 5. That means people were very satisfied with her work. I looked at her past earnings through Elance too. That helps show how often she's worked in this system. She had earned $178.00 which was very low. Still, there were other people with no ratings and no earnings. I looked a bit deeper into Amanda's ratings and found she's done two jobs. I clicked on her portfolio to see some examples of her work.

The next step was to send her a message by email. I requested a video call meeting on Skype. This helps me make a decision. I always do the same thing when I'm picking someone through Elance. I choose the two or three people whose offers I like. Then I send a message to them saying let's talk on Skype. Even if I have the full profile of this person, with all their stats, a quick chat clarifies. I see if this person speaks the right sort of English, has the skill sets I want, and has the culture match for me.

My Global Dynamic Team

Right now I have a team of over 30 people I hire on the Global Dynamic Team model basis. I delegate almost everything to them! They're critical to my business now and I don't have a multi-million dollar payroll to take care of.

I make sure I see as many of them as possible on a video Skype call. I find this better aligns my personality and qualities with my freelancers. I have a rule to say I don't want anybody on my team who I don't look forward to talking to.

That might be a little bit too picky for some people. But I figure life's too short to be working with people I don't like. If I dread talking to them and think, "I'm going to be drained by this energy vampire again. I just hate dealing with this person," then I don't hire them. I hire freelancers who are terrific fun to talk to and offer a terrific project rate. You don't have to settle because there are so many skilled workers when you open yourself up to a global labor force. You don't have to compromise your happiness or the entrepreneurial culture you're looking to create. There are tons of workers which means you can choose one who fits well with you.

When I click '*Select*', the website takes me through to the payment section, and it asks me to pay for the job. The really great thing about Elance is if you put a payment in for a job, it puts your money in escrow. In other words, you're not paying the worker directly, you're paying Elance. That way the worker knows that the money is available to pay them, but they don't get it until the job is done to your satisfaction. Then you release it from Elance to the freelancer.

If you're not totally satisfied with the job, and for whatever reason the worker can't or won't fix the problem, then you can cancel the payment. Elance gives you your money back. Otherwise you can talk to Elance and raise what's called a dispute if you have any problems.

Elance is a very low risk way of getting work done piece by piece even on an ongoing basis. It's easy to find the people you need and the Elance system makes it a secure working environment.

Deeper Insights into the World of Elance

Once you've posted an ad, you can select a criterion such as; *I only want people to see this who are in North America or Australia.* You can limit those who see your ad based on their geography. If you only want to hire an Englishman you can choose 'England' and Elance only allows workers in England to see it. You can set the ad to be active for the number of days you choose like three days, or five days. What I find is within the course of couple of hours, or certainly within the course of couple of days, I get replies from people who'd like to do the job.

They tell me the amount of money they'll charge, setting their own fee. This is beautiful because they tell me how much they want me to pay them. I get to choose how much I want to pay based on the responses.

I often get 10 or 15 people applying before I pull down the ad. I don't want 50 people applying because it's too many to dig through. This group of 10 or 15 people is enough for me to look through, especially because it shows they jumped on it quickly. I like to hire go-getters who respond and deliver quickly.

Once they apply, I look at 5 or 10 criterion of how Elance organizes workers. I can see how much money they've made on Elance, in other words if they've made zero dollars it means they really don't know the system yet. I prefer someone who's made $5,000 or $10,000 or $50,000, who really knows how to work virtually.

They get ratings, reference comments from previous Elance employers and of course they have a substantial portfolio. So if it's a designer, I can see their work. If it's a lawyer, I can read their reports. If it's a bookkeeper, I can see what other people have said about them, how trustworthy they are and how well they work.

Now understand, even with all of this data, occasionally I hire people who don't pan out. You can hire in parallel if you need to. It's just the same as hiring for full-time or part time because sometimes the first person doesn't work out. It may take a little more time to find the right person.

On the flip side, they're able to see your record in Elance. They see how many people you've hired, how much feedback you've left, how many projects you've posted, and how much money you've spent over time so they get a feeling for you as an employer.

As on Fiverr you have a little mailbox where you get to correspond with each other. You can send files and communicate whatever the job needs to get done.

I get all kinds of creative work done for generally a few hundred dollars at a time instead of thousands or tens of thousands. So you can now imagine the power at your fingertips to get a product or a service started. Instantly you have a skilled team available to you to do substantial creative, design, bookkeeping, and every part of the business. For the small things you invest $10.00, $50.00 or $100.00. For the bigger things it's a couple hundred dollars at a time. Before you know it you have an extraordinary team of people to support you piece by piece as you're exploring your new ideas. You rule out the losers. You run big and scale up the winners. You do this risking only a few hundred dollars instead of the hundreds of thousands in the past. You can get at least a prototype designed fast. And this happens with the minimum frustration a new product or service can have.

Example / Hiring A Professional Musician for Pennies

Here is the transcript (yep, I hired a freelancer to transcribe this) of a conversation between me and my business partner Clint, which might answer some of your questions.

Clint: Right, let's talk about some of the key specifics. I want to hire a service. Let's say I want to hire a two minute guitar solo. I don't even know if that's possible on Elance.

Tim: Oh, absolutely.

Clint: What would I write in the job posting? What key specifics would get that good result that I'm looking for?

Tim: Here is a generalization for you. It turns out that the creative industries in particular, say musicians, artists, and writers, are generally not well remunerated. I think there is truth to the cliché about starving artists so you tend to find extraordinary experienced musicians, artists, writers, designers, illustrators through websites like Fiverr and Elance. Certainly I see people saying things about chords, songs, or jingles. You'll find all sorts of people who do that on Fiverr for five dollars in which case you just pick a gig, jump in and get something recorded. In the case of Elance, let's do an example.

Clint: How about getting a bass guitar track done?

Tim: Great. What you do is get on to Elance. You log into your account and you hit '*Post' a job.* It's the little green button top right hand on the screen. It then pops up a window that allows you to type. I'd start by talking about the **talent you want**. So you write '*I'm looking for a fantastic bass guitar player, someone who knows their way around a Gibson*'. Clint, I don't even know what a Gibson is so I'm just making that up.

Clint: It's some kind of brand of a guitar. That's all I know.

Tim: All right, someone who knows their way around a Gibson, that's the talent that you're looking for. Now let's say that I'm interested in a specific genre. So you write '*I want to get a two minute bass guitar track recorded in the jazz style that makes me sound cool as I talk about my product.*'

Now I've explained the talents and I've outlined the gig as specifically as possible. The next thing I'll talk about is **experience**. So I write '*I want someone who has at least five years of experience as bass guitar player and who's been gigging around North America for all of that time.*' That's nice and specific.

The last thing you want is to write something about **culture**. So you could write 'I want someone who is relaxed, creative and easy to work with, who loves music and would be happy to help me with this project. '

Now you've written **talent, experience and culture**, and sometimes I write a little **about me**. I'd say, I'm a young entrepreneur based in Austin, Texas in North America. I have this great project about underwater pantomiming. All it needs is a great jam track. That is all you need to write, just three to six sentences.

I mean, it's insanely simple. Three sentences and three hours later you can have six bass guitar players saying they're interested in helping you. It's staggeringly efficient.

Clint: So, anything else?

Tim: Right. Now down the bottom, before you hit '*Post*', it says; "*Do you want any advanced options?*" I always click on that option and a list of options drops down.

First, you specify the skill sets you're looking for. In this case probably music, instrumental bass player or something like that. If it's a lawyer, it's a specific kind of lawyer. If it's design, you can say, "*can use Photoshop*". If it's accounting you might say, "*can use Quicken*" or whatever system you want them to use.

You specify skill sets then under that you can specify, if you wish, where this person comes from.

You say, *I want this thing to be live in three days* and you hit '*Post*'. That allows you to review the post and you hit '*go*'.

It doesn't matter if there's not enough detail because **you can add detail to the proposal later.** For example, you might have ten people apply and one person says "*I'll do it for 50 bucks*" and another person says "*I'll do it for one thousand*". You might add something that says, *I'm looking to pay around about a hundred dollars for this* if you wanted to, but you don't have to. You might add something like, *I forgot to say in the style of Michael Jackson,* or whatever you figure out later.

Once you've posted, people just apply saying, "*I'd love to do this*". Again, you might ask for examples but most often I just have a look at their portfolio and have a little listen.

Clint: OK, now what?

Tim: OK. Now I'll generally get between ten and twenty people applying to work with me within a few days. I often get the first five or ten people within two or three *hours*.

Next step, I try to narrow down to a final three using the criterion I mentioned to you before. How many jobs have they done, what are their ratings, how are their testimonials, what are their portfolios like, and how much money they've already earned.

I always narrow it down to three and I post them and say, "Hi, you're in my final three, but before I choose the final person, is there a chance we can chat by Skype?"

Now, the reason I do this Clint, is I figure, if you haven't mastered Skype, particularly video Skype, then you don't really know how to work virtually. Do you agree? Skype is an essential tool.

Clint: Absolutely, it's free, there's no reason why you wouldn't be using it.

Tim: Exactly, it's free, it has a great audio and video connection, so why wouldn't you use it? So I chat to my final three and narrow it down to one. So by the time you had a bit of a chat, and a bit of talk about jazz and maybe they have a bit of a riff, you can probably figure out which freelancer you want to actually take. There's another big green button which says 'award job to this person', so you hit, Elance asks you to fund the job and suddenly the gig goes live. Boom. It's on.

Clint: So on Elance you get to talk with them whereas on Fiverr you don't.

Tim: Absolutely true. In Fiverr, you don't even know their name. I mean it really is odd. I now know one of my transcribers is called Kiko and one of them is called Denise and one is called Debbie, but all I saw was their nicknames until they chose to reveal their names to me. If you try to put your email address for private contact, I think Fiverr deletes it.

Clint: It gives you a digital hand slap for sure.

Tim: They don't want you to go out of the Fiverr system, and frankly why would you? It's such a secure, excellent low cost system. I can't imagine why you'd go out of it because I think it's better and safer to stay in it. I'm sure someone has figured out how to get out of it but I frankly stay in it. Also, I am so grateful to Elance that why would I go out of this system? I wouldn't have the chance to give this person a great review and do all of those positive things. I generally stay inside both those systems with the exception as I say, of Skype, and the communication that helps me decide who I should work with.

I figure Elance and Fiverr have both earned their cut and more, so I'm delighted to continue to use them.

Extra / The Next Revolution

There's one more thing I want to mention. It's the next revolution. It's on the way, my friends – so get ready for change! Let me explain.

Let's start with the 1st recent revolution that happened in the book publishing industry.

Just ten years ago if you were to write a book, you'd have to get a publisher because who can afford to run 5,000 or 10,000 copies in a speculative way, right?

Then new technology allowed you to print out a single copy of a book instead of that huge print run. They called it *"print-on-demand"*. Now you can print one book just as easily as you can print 10,000 with the same level of quality at a very good price.

You don't need the publisher in the same way anymore. The price of publishing came down to cents on the dollar compared to what it was before.

Next came the music industry. When I first worked with CDs, for example, I needed to run 1,000 copies to get the price down low enough to make a profit. Now you can run a single copy for the same price. And, to be honest, you can make it happen more cheaply online.

Next came the television industry. Again, back in the day I had to run at least 1,000 DVDs to make the exercise profitable. Now I can run a single DVD with the same level of quality and the same low cost.

So it happened with books, CDs and DVDs. It has happened online, of course, bringing the cost of publishing information down to almost nothing.

Now it's happening with manufacturing.

Let me explain. If I wanted to make, for example, a mobile phone case a few years back, I had to design it, make molds and do a multi-thousand dollar plastic injection molding run just for a slim chance at a profit.

Now you can do one using a new desktop technology.

This next revolution is called *3D printing*. Many people don't even know this exists. You can now buy a desktop printer that prints out an item.

You heard me. It doesn't print paper, it prints out physical items. Whatever you can think of you can now print out. Print out a cup. Print out a bowl. Print out a figurine of your favorite movie character.

These items can be made of plastic, metals, ceramics, and more. They can be printed out *in multiple colors*. You can print three dimensional objects pretty much the same way you print a flat piece of paper. I don't want to give you the impression you can print any 3D object imaginable, but people are printing out amazing things. This week people are printing out prosthetic limbs. People are printing, and take a moment to understand how this is going to effect the world, cars. You can get a printer big enough and sophisticated enough to print out your car.

Now it's very early on in this revolution so printing out a car is in the developmental stages. You can't just print out a Ford Focus, for example. It's happening, though – in the early stages.

For example, on Season 6, episode 14 of The Big Bang Theory TV show, the characters Howard and Raj printed out action figures of themselves.

3D printing has gone mainstream media. This is great for small and even large retailers. It's great for you to test out a new physical product idea. If you've got a comic book with lots of action figures, instead of stocking all the characters, you can just print them when a customer is standing before you requesting one. Or the customer orders from your website, you print the action figure, then ship it to your customer.

Example / Idea to Market in One Week -- the Ray Gun

Let me give you an example from this week. I mentioned this one earlier in the book.

I had an idea this past weekend for making a steam-punk ray-gun to sell to the Comic.con market when talking with my friend Robin. So I took five minutes and sketched something out.

Then, on Monday morning before I starting consulting with a CEO client, I posted a job on Elance. It was about six sentences long – here it is.

3D Model and Print Genius

Hello!

I'm looking for someone to help me in the 3D
model and print world. I have some ideas /
sketches that I'd like build into a 3D model
that we could then upload for printing to a
site like Shapeways, Ponoko or Sculpteo. Or,
in the event that we do lots of this work,
directly into a 3D printer. You might even
have your own 3D printer ..

I'd like to start by sending a single sketch
or a ray gun (a little obvious, I know) to be
modeled. Can you help?

Oh - and it goes without saying that you're
fun, relaxed and easy to work with.

Looking forward to getting in touch,

Tim

After posting this, I went away and spent the day with my client. The next morning, I had 5 or 10 proposals. I spoke with a great guy from Serbia and he agreed to do the job. About 3 hours later I had a 3D model ready to print on Ponoko. The whole new business idea has cost me $32.88 so far. I'll run some copies, put a page on my site, advertise through Facebook for nothing and see what people think. That's <u>level one</u> ready to rock. Easy, right?!

Upending the Manufacturing World

B3D (before 3D printing), you'd need expensive prototype design, to source plastics, plastic injection molding, and that wasn't even worth doing unless you're making thousands. For metals, milling complicated manufacturing costs a ton. A lot of these past dreams are now economically and financially feasible to test because of 3D printing technology. There are a number of websites that own a 3D printer for you like Ponoko, Thingiverse or Scultpeo.

You just pay them a small fee to print your 3D object instead of having to shell out $2,000 to buy your own printer. There are also local print options. You can have it printed in China and sent to you. The beauty is you can print-on-demand, one at a time at a low cost. When you figure out what works, you can order the quantity you need to satisfy demand. And it'll be shipped to you in a timely fashion. In some cases your physical objects will be packaged and ready for sale.

What's really nice is this whole new makers' movement has sprung up. They often have studios, little manufacturing factories in cities and in many major cities you can go play with this stuff. You don't shell out to buy the equipment. They have the plastics, metals or other raw materials required to create the finished product. And they add the value of people who are already interested and already competent to help you. These more experienced users can advise you and tell you what traps you're falling into. They can tell you if something you're doing isn't technologically possible yet to save you time instead of chasing an unfeasible idea. So you don't have to go the old model of large scale manufacturing even for physical products.

This social help is invaluable. Having someone else figure out the kinks in a project saves you from wasting time and getting frustrated. This is a huge boost. Also, starting from the midpoint, or at least not at the starting line, is so valuable to a new business idea. Why not start part way through the race instead of at the beginning?

If you start scaling a successful physical object, then buying your own 3D printer may be a positive ROI (return on investment). They've got one out now called the Replicator which is probably $2,000 instead of the $10,000 models. Just do a little online research, talk to your local or regional makers' movement contacts and see what model is the fit for your purpose and project.

I'd only consider purchasing a 3D printer for ideas that have graduated to <u>level three</u> businesses. It's too risky and not worth the investment otherwise.

So now you can set up your own factory right on your desk. Seriously. It's amazing. You've got a whole world of previously out of reach ideas now possible to test. The technology is there to test them and it's advanced enough to where it's affordable to do so.

I don't know if it's Aldous Huxley's Brave New World. But it's fascinating technology that continues to advance, bringing costs down and expanding possibilities.

Bringing this System Together

So here are your new habits.

1. Build your business by conducting **entrepreneurial experiments** according to the Levels and Pricing processes

2. Change your way of thinking from the Hierarchical to the **Global Dynamic Team model**

3. Build your Global Dynamic Team using tools like **MTurk.com, Fiverr.com** and **Elance.com**

4. Leverage your Global Dynamic Team according to the golden rule.

Remember the golden rule.

"For everything you love to do, do it. For everything else, delegate!"
Tim Levy.

Wrapping Up

Now, let's say you have read this book, and you enjoyed the concepts. You've embraced the tools to take the process of entrepreneurial development of new products and services.

Just to recap, these tools:

- Take out much of the risk of development.

- Take out much of the time you might spend

- Take out a huge amount of money you might have needed in the past.

As I've said I prefer to apply the tools gently over time to get things right, but maybe you decide to do things in a hurry.

Let's say you've started experimenting and made some money.

Some people get a little bit too excited at this stage. They get a little bit too attached to a product, and put a ton of time in doing it before it's proven in the market.

Remember, there's only one way to figure out how much to charge for something – ask the market! There's only one way to figure out which features and benefits are important – ask the market! It's not about what's in *your* head. It's not about what *you* think. It's about what the market thinks, feels and buys.

Now you have the tools and concepts to build your own lightning quick, super cheap team to delegate to.

Transitioning - What Is It? Why Is It Important?

I want to tell you a cautionary tale. It's the story of someone who quits their job to follow their dream of making... let's say .. a children's book series. Or maybe it's to start their own clothing line. Or maybe it's to start their own service business.

Either way, abandoning your current source of income for something so risky is asking for trouble. You know how the story goes, right? The person leaps too soon, runs out of money and has to go get a job again. Along the way, they lose belief in themselves as entrepreneurs.

Instead, the trick is to *transition.* Let me explain in a little more detail.

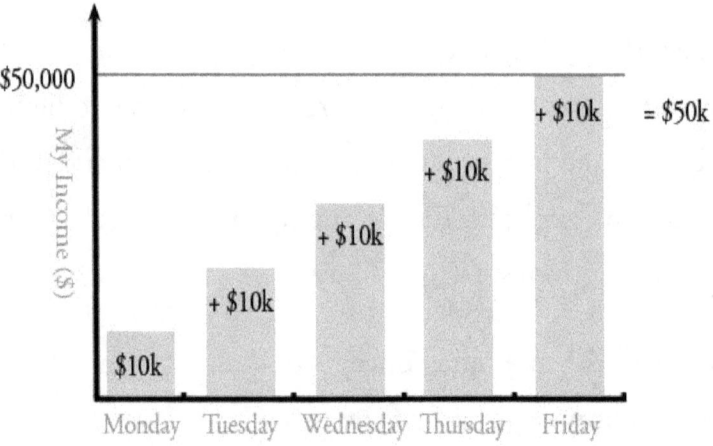

Transitioning from One Source of Income to Another

Let's say you're doing a job and earning $50,000 a year. To earn this, you work from Monday to Friday. This means all your Mondays combine to bring in $10,000. All the Tuesdays combine to bring in $10,000, and so on. This adds up to the year's salary.

What I say is rather than quit your job and go from $50,000 a year to living by blowing through your savings staggeringly quickly, why not slow down a bit. You could say, *I will take my job from five days a week to four days a week when I have started consistently earning what will add up to ten thousand dollars a year from my new project.*

This means the new project must bring in $10,000 a year or $10,000 / 12 = a bit under $1,000 a month.

Once you've earned $1,000 a month from your new products for three or six months, that's enough for you to feel it's a healthy trend. At this point, you might go to your boss and say, "I'd like to take this full-time job down to four days a week."

If you're more efficient by outsourcing your own job to Fiverr or Elance by managing your own teams, you should be able to keep the level of work constant. When you put in your request, you'll get any of a variety of outcomes.

- Some bosses will say, "Cool, fine I don't care if you report four days a week."

- Other people would want you five days in the office a week, so taking a day off a week is not always an option.

- What if you offer to take a commensurate pay cut? While still turning in five days' worth of work, while showing up at the office for only four days?

- Often, people will say, "Really? Seriously you'll be coming in four days a week and doing five days' worth of work and you'll take $40,000 instead of $50,000?"

Once you've started using and profiting from this system, it's a good idea to make a *very conservative* transition. Now you'll be earning $10,000 per annum for a level two entrepreneurial idea, and $40,000 by working four days a week (say, Monday to Thursday) at your job. So, you're still earning the $50,000 you need in order to thrive.

Now, with more time, you can earn the next $10,000 and buy back your Thursday. So, you'll be working Monday to Wednesday at the job, and Thursday and Friday at the entrepreneurial ideas.

Next, you buy back your Wednesday and then your Tuesday and finally, your Monday.

Using this system, you're not taking a huge risk or leaping off the income cliff. You're not getting too excited. You're building up your entrepreneurial ideas and experience and income until such time that you can afford to transition comfortably out of full-time. You go to possibly part-time employment and then into pursuing your entrepreneurial ideas full-time if you choose. You're in command of your life's direction.

I want to be clear that this is not the way for everyone. Not everyone gets to do this complete transition, but I'm sitting here as a living example of someone who has.

Example / Clint Goes Off-the-Cliff

My partner Clint on the other hand, took the leap-off-the-cliff method. It worked for him and he's now in his own business.

As he says, "Yeah, I got to a point with my job working for a state agency where I just said I was having some pretty terrible thoughts. I got to end this for myself! So, I got out of that and started doing more of what I care about. I was a single guy with no family so I was risking only my own comfort but even still this (transitioning) is a much preferred way."

Get Started!

That's really the way I would close up any conversation about this system. I consider the best way is to be financially conservative. I'm not a massive risk taker, which is why I like to spend time developing things properly. Many people are much quicker and less conservative than I am, but I consider it a strength to do things slowly and well, to take the time to find where your genuine value is. It takes time for me to bring true value into the world, figuring out the right form and the right price.

Fast or slower, now you have these tools to make it staggeringly inexpensive. You don't have to own the skill sets anymore, and you don't have to know how to put your own website online. You just have to hire someone on Fiverr or Elance to do it for you. You don't have to know how to write a children's script. You just have to know how to find someone who can. That is now the work-on-demand.

You know you can find that person with a few sentences and after a couple of hours in Elance you're ready to go with your entrepreneurial project. You can get it made up, start generating income and transition gently over the course of time. You keep your current source of income during the transition so you're never at risk. At every point you're moving closer to exclusively doing the things you love to do rather than the things you feel you have to do.

Clint and I talked all this over a little while ago. Here's a poignant snippet from our conversation. Allow it to help you transition.

Clint: You mention one very important point about being conservative and doing things that are at a high quality level even though it takes longer. It really goes towards your online reputation.

Tim: Look, it's absolutely true. I think there's no substitute for genuine value. You know, I can only highly recommend people that take the time to do it right, to make sure they're delivering genuine value and that they're actually doing something helpful and useful. It does take a little time to do that but it's worth it in the end.

Clint: So you're saying that it's walking that tightrope in between working things out with strangers as you're doing and the paralysis of perfectionism that would be the flip side of the coin.

Tim: Perfectionism really is a trap for the rookie entrepreneur. My sample story here was Steven Spielberg. I know that Steven Spielberg is *the* movie making genius of our time but it turns out that his first movies were … not great. I'm not trying to judge Steven Spielberg but I understand his first movie simply wasn't as good as his second. His second wasn't as good as his third and his tenth and his twentieth. You have to do those ones knowing that you're getting better and better every time. Why be stressed about trying to create perfection when you're simply not in a position to access it? Why not instead say, "Listen, what I'm doing is a series of better and better drafts that I'm refining with constant feedback from the market."

That's why this system is not about perfectionism. Instead it's about experimentation combined with feedback to move constantly closer to excellence.

I make sure people know that what they're doing is getting things to market quickly, inexpensively and effectively to see what the market thinks. After all, how do you even know what perfect is? It's your clients who decide, not you.

Clint: Right, any final thoughts to wrap the book?

Tim: I have found real personal satisfaction in being entrepreneurial. I love bringing new ideas into the world and helping other people do that too, but it isn't for the faint of heart. It isn't for people who give up quickly, or those who are overwhelmed by fear or failure. It's for the strong, the creative, the engaged; it's for the people who work hard and are passionate about living their dreams.

You get out there and do it. It's just like any other skill, like the first time you get in the car. You look at all the steering wheels and levers and pins and things, and think, "I'll never be able to do this!" But before long you're driving along without thinking about it at all. These tools, processes and ways of thinking might be a little alien at first but after a while you reach for them just as easily as you drive a car and reach for the phone. They just become a way of life.

The entrepreneur must be willing to risk a little bit of TV time and invest a little bit of money to test out these ideas quickly and find the winners. It's a revelation for most people, to find out it's possible to start a business idea for $50.00 or $100.00. You can get it online and have other people help you if you don't have that expertise yourself. And you do it for the kind of money you use to buy snacks for your home party on Super Bowl Sunday.

Instead of hosting that Super Bowl party, you can put that money into your project and attend someone else's Super Bowl party, and that's the bottom line. Or else you *can* host a party, invite a whole bunch of people and then pitch them your entrepreneurial idea and raise money at halftime!

Any Questions?

I hope your mind is exploding with possibilities as I've revealed to you all the sneaky, quick, inexpensive ways I get things done day to day.

You can now test your ideas quickly and cheaply. You can get the marketing collateral, audio products, video products, free images, and books that you're going to use created at these websites.

To market and scale your winning projects you'll want to get the full video walkthrough program. I go through the steps showing you my screen. You'll see the tools in here and more.

Entrepreneur's Toolkit video program here:

http://www.timlevy.net

Contact

If you have any questions or thoughts, please feel free to get in touch directly: email gamble@thelifesummit.com, and let me know what you're thinking. Ask any questions you might have and I'll do my best to see them answered.

Thanks so much for your time! I hope this has been tremendously helpful for you and has made sense for you and brought lots of energy and creativity into your day.

Yours,

Tim

About the Author

Tim Levy is a writer, speaker, consultant and coach. He spends most of his time helping CEOs with clarity, strategy, mindset and technology. He routinely speaks for peak organizations like Vistage International, CEOSpace International and Secret Knock.

He's available via his web site at www.timlevy.net

Other Recent Titles Include ..

Available online at www.timlevy.net

Tim Levy
Clarity is everything

Home   About Tim   Coaching   Writing   Speaking   Blog   Shop   Contact   Login

Welcome To Timlevy.net

Tim Levy is an author, speaker, consultant and coach. He works with CEOs and entrepreneurs on clarity, strategy and mindset. He routinely speaks for peak organizations like Vistage International, CEOSpace International and Secret Knock. He has a particular focus on web technology and digital content, including books, CDs, online training and broadcast television. His clients report transformational shifts and rapid growth in their business and personal lives.

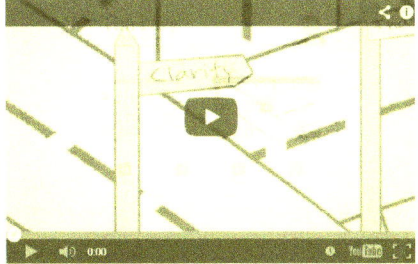

Coaching

Writing

Speaking

Shopping

Books

Please visit me at www.timlevy.net

Is there more I can do?

If there's any way I can help you further, then let's talk. Please call, email me directly or via *Contact Us* on the site I'll see what I can do.

Tim Levy and Associates LLC

Based In | Austin, Texas

Telephone | (512) 782 4401

Email | creativity@timlevy.net

Web | www.timlevy.net

www.ingramcontent.com/pod-product-compliance
Lightning Source LLC
Chambersburg PA
CBHW051711170526
45167CB00002B/629